PARANORMAL UNCENSORED: A RAW LOOK AT LOUISIANA GHOST HUNTING

PARANORMAL UNCENSORED: A RAW LOOK AT LOUISIANA GHOST HUNTING

BRAD DUPLECHIEN

iUniverse, Inc.
New York Bloomington Shanghai

PARANORMAL UNCENSORED:
A RAW LOOK AT LOUISIANA GHOST HUNTING

Copyright © 2008 by Brad Duplechien

All rights reserved. No part of this book may be used or reproduced by any means, graphic, electronic, or mechanical, including photocopying, recording, taping or by any information storage retrieval system without the written permission of the publisher except in the case of brief quotations embodied in critical articles and reviews.

iUniverse books may be ordered through booksellers or by contacting:

iUniverse
1663 Liberty Drive
Bloomington, IN 47403
www.iuniverse.com
1-800-Authors (1-800-288-4677)

Because of the dynamic nature of the Internet, any Web addresses or links contained in this book may have changed since publication and may no longer be valid.

The views expressed in this work are solely those of the author and do not necessarily reflect the views of the publisher, and the publisher hereby disclaims any responsibility for them.

ISBN: 978-0-595-51265-2 (pbk)
ISBN: 978-0-595-61828-6 (ebk)

Printed in the United States of America

This book is dedicated to my wife, Erin, daughter, Olivia, and new son, Michael, who was born the week this book was completed. Thank you so much for having the patience to put up with all the "ghost crap." I love you always. Also, to my mom and dad, thanks for always being so supportive in all that I have strived for.

CONTENTS

ACKNOWLEDGEMENTS.................................ix
FOREWORD BY JEANNE FROIS.........................xi
INTRODUCTION.....................................xiii

1   LET'S START AT THE BEGINNING....................1
2   FT. DERUSSY CEMETERY (MARKSVILLE, LA)...........9
3   LOUISIANA FOLKLORE.............................19
4   GHOST HUNTING 101..............................27
5   TOOLS OF THE TRADE.............................39
6   THE MAKING OF A GHOST HUNTER...................50
7   THE JONES'S RESIDENCE (LEESVILLE, LA)..........60
8   INTERESTING CHARACTERS.........................73
9   OAK ALLEY PLANTATION (VACHERIE, LA)............83
10   THE BIRTH OF LOUISIANA SPIRITS.................94
11   THE SHREVEPORT MUNICIPAL AUDITORIUM (SHREVEPORT, LA)...............................105
12   JOSEPH JEFFERSON MANSION (NEW IBERIA, LA).....114
13   DERIDDER GOTHIC JAIL (DERIDDER, LA)...........124

14	WAVERLY HILLS TUBERCULOSIS SANATORIUM (LOUISVILLE, KY) 139
15	DIRTY TACTICS 154
16	WHAT THE FUTURE HOLDS 164

REFERENCES... 169

WEBSITES.. 171

ACKNOWLEDGEMENTS

I would like to thank all of the members of LaSpirits for all their hard work and dedication. Without them, there would have never even been a group and for that, I am truly grateful. Despite many of the highs and lows, you have continued to work diligently in keeping our group the most reputable in the state. Thanks to Brandon, Steve, and Elissa for hanging in there from day one. Special thanks to Jennifer Broussard for all the time and effort she has put forth, running the group during my absences. I seriously doubt we could have accomplished near as much if you weren't in the group.

Another special acknowledgement goes out to Jeanne Frois. Jeanne was kind enough to take us serious, featuring the group in an article for Louisiana Life Magazine in 2006. The article was a huge success, as we were then featured in another issue in 2007 and a great cover story for the New Orleans Gambit. Of all the writers I have worked with, I have been most impressed with Jeanne's work. I thought that it would only be fitting that Jeanne write the Foreword to this book, as her work is simply amazing, captivating the readers, truly enveloping them in the subject matter.

I would also like to thank the following friends, former members, and media personalities for their continued service and support of the group: Jason Ponthieux, Raymond Chandler, Todd & Korrin Weaver, Tiffany Romero, Marti Bordelon, Bill Murphy, Thomas Durant, LJ Geilen, Rebecca Jarred, Kristyn Gartland, Judy Smythe, Amy Bruni (API), Mark Stinson (Ghost Vigil), the entire TAPS Family, Al Tyas, Christy Selfridge (OKPRI), Susan Stevenson, Duana Trotter, Shawn Martin, Hattie Sherrick, Dawn Provost, Lori Veazy, Zeb Mayhew, Mike Richard, Jill Kuhn, Steve Mayeux, Elaine Coleman, Teresa Micheels, Mike Carson, Alyne Pustanio, Brian Heffron (The Blue Meanie), and last but not least, Golden Needle Monograms for making us look so damn good.

Most importantly, I would like to thank each and every individual that has ever spoken an ill-word about me or LaSpirits. Always remember that it was your negativity that forced me to strive even harder to get this group where it is today. To all those who have lied, been two-faced, and conniving to us: This book is for you.

FOREWORD

BY JEANNE FROIS

The first thing that made me trust Brad Duplechien from the moment I approached him about a story for my regular feature, "Around Louisiana," in Louisiana Life Magazine, was that he didn't trust me.

Unlike a large number of people who the media approaches, Brad did not fall all over me in eagerness to get his story written. On behalf of himself and his fellow members of LaSpirits Paranormal Investigations, Brad expressed legitimate concerns about my interest in his work. I admired that. Personally knowing the sting of plagiarism, I identified with their fear that I would record the group's experiences as my own. I understood their concern that I might possibly be writing to denigrate, make fun, and pass them off to the public as kooks. Prior to contacting Brad, I had already visited the excellent website of LaSpirits and came away most impressed by their professionalism. I felt reassured they were legitimate due to the fact that most of their investigations debunked reported hauntings in Louisiana. They employed a scientific, rational approach to what many would consider a hysterical subject. There were a few tales of ghosts, however, that couldn't be debunked and those were the ones I wanted to write about.

For each autumn edition, the good publisher and editors of Louisiana Life Magazine, Errol Laborde, Morgan Packard and Eve Kidd Crawford indulge my never outgrown penchant for Halloween. They cut me loose upon the Bayou State and allow me to write of reported hauntings and other things that are knee deep in Louisiana weird. My prerequisite for writing about them is that they must be based in unexplainable fact. My goal is to find tales of hauntings experienced by rational, down to earth people that are non-sensationalistic, valid and unexplainable.

The courtesy, humor and utter professionalism of Brad and LaSpirits fit the bill entirely for me. I was, therefore, quite flattered when Brad asked me to write the foreword to his delightful book. We both share a deep abiding love for Louisiana, have roots in Central Louisiana, and have experienced separate personal paranormal events in our past. Both of us know that not everything strange can be considered paranormal or supernatural.

In that crazy tongue-in-cheek movie, "The Mummy Returns," I often fall over laughing when one of the bandits on the train accuses an Egyptian of thinking, "this is cursed, that is cursed," meaning that everything has a mark on it according to ancient lore. Humorously written by Brad, you'll see in this book that there are some people involved in paranormal investigations who hold a similar erroneous belief.

So ignore any bumps in the night you may hear for the moment, settle down and delve into this humorous, frequently atmospheric little tome of ghost hunting that is part how-to manual and part personal history told in Brad's own unique voice. With some Louisiana folklore thrown in for good measure along with downright ghostly experiences, it chronicles the fascinating adventures and expertise of a very down-to-earth young man with a most unusual hobby.

INTRODUCTION

It appears that in this day and age, everyone is hopping aboard the paranormal bandwagon, looking at a way to make it big and make a few dollars. Sure, it would be quite nice to make some extra cash, yet I do have a legitimate reason for writing this book. Needless to say, I am one of the most passionate people when it comes to the field of the paranormal. I, like most paranormal addicts, spend many afternoons in the paranormal section of our local bookstore, flipping through the same books time and time again. Sure, many of the books are very good reads, yet after the first five, the titles just seem to get monotonous, all covering the same subject matter, never straying from the mainstream. Determined to look for different avenues in putting out an interesting, yet informative read, I had to look no further than ourselves.

We are bombarded on a daily basis with "reality" television shows which, in all actuality, have as much reality as an honest politician. At any given time, there are at least five reality shows out there either pitting contestants against each other or putting "real people" in a house together, but the truth of the matter is, it's all staged. Producers filter through thousands of applicants, purposely finding individuals with completely different personalities with one sole purpose: to watch them fight like cats and dogs. Even in regards to the media, things are often sugar-coated to portray things in a light that they feel appropriate.

When I began to plan the layout for this book I debated on which route I should take. Sure, with the amount of experience I have in the paranormal I could produce a traditional book, covering some of the most interesting locations in Louisiana, while giving a crash course on investigating. Yet, as always, being the envelope-pusher that I am, the traditional just wasn't going to cut it for me. My layout then shifted to taking the traditional and modifying things a little, allowing readers to get a closer look at some of the kooky individuals who can make up the hobby. Unfortunately, my job description on my income taxes says "Federal Correctional Officer", not "Paranormal Investigator." This is, and always will be, a hobby and a hobby is supposed to be fun. On many occasions, I have been accused of making a mockery of the hobby with immature antics and so forth, yet these accusations often come from those who simply think negative on a daily basis. Regardless, no one will be able to argue the truth and the truth is exactly what I will bring to you and believe it or not, when the smoke clears, you may actually get an awesome history lesson on one of the most intriguing states in the country when it comes to paranormal investigating.

I wanted to create a book that was comprised of all the things I enjoyed from other books I had read, capturing the different interests of a broad range of people. This book will cover a wide array of subject matter such as rare Louisiana folk lore, a how-to in modern paranormal investigating, tours of some great haunted Louisiana locations, and an overall rough look at a hobby that is usually portrayed as a harmonious unit.

Those of you who have watched a season or two of any given paranormal-related television show and feel that you want to try it for yourself; I will be quick to tell you that what you see on television is not how it is in reality. People just don't realize the amount of drama and headache there is in the paranormal community. Sure, I may not be that old, but I have never, in all of my life, witnessed such dirty tactics, debauchery, lying, and fraud, until I joined a group. Hopefully, by reading this, the newcomers will learn from our mistakes and enjoy this field for the great hobby that it is, while keeping the veterans humble by reminding them of some of the stupid antics that goes on in a field that contain probably some of the most unique personalities in existence.

To avoid any legal retribution on my already broke rear end, the actual names concerning these former associates have been changed and some specific identifying details have been omitted. What I will do is simply take you on a journey of what I have been through to get my group where we are today. Some of it is hilarious; some of it will relight a flame in my rear, making me madder than a dog passing tacks all over again. However, when the smoke clears, you will see how the tough times were, in fact, the fuel that caused me to be more determined than ever to see our group succeed in being the most reputable investigative group in Louisiana.

—*"Laissez Les Bons Temps Roulez"* (Let the Good Times Roll.)

1
LET'S START AT THE BEGINNING

I guess the best place to start is to explain what got me interested in such a strange hobby. I was born in the small town of Mansura, Louisiana, with a population of "not many". My mom had me when she was almost thirty. She herself was born when her parents were quite old. This resulted in me spending most of my days hanging around the old folk. Mansura was not a very happening place. Besides the good ole Roy Theater and the snowball stand, you really didn't have much to do. About the most excitement I can remember growing up was when my cousin and I would make my great-aunt mad by smashing all the tomatoes in her garden. We were such brats growing up, as I can remember us purposely clogging toilets in department stores, watching them overflow and going to grocery stores, poking our fingers in all of the packs of ground meat. Looking back, if my children would act like that I would threaten to kill them.

Summers were always the worst when I was growing up, as I was forced to go with my mother and grandmother and visit all the older aunts and uncles, which consisted of sitting there in a house with no air conditioner, while they babbled back and forth in French, watching soap operas and drinking coffee. I swear, I never saw people drink so much damned coffee. As mentioned, all they spoke was French with each other because even to this day, Creole French is often spoken in the southern portion of Louisiana. My uncle, who is only in his sixties, did not learn to speak English until he was around eight years old because in those days, French was the language taught in school, not to mention that is the only language your parents spoke as well.

Cajuns are truly unique people, living in a dying part of Louisiana culture. I really could not see being anything else other than a "Coonass". The term "Coonass" is often looked at as a derogatory label, except if you are one of course. No one truly knows where the term came from, yet a legitimate Coonass will hold his head high when identified as one. In one interesting story, I once heard that the term originated from Cajun soldiers stationed in France. When the French soldiers heard these Cajuns speaking such a broken form of "their language", they quickly turned their noses towards them, calling them *Coon-ase*, which roughly translated into a "dirty whore". Of course, being the rowdy Cajuns that we are, we took that label and wore it with pride. Coonasses are very easy going, always looking for a reason to have a get-together. You can bet that if you have food and beer in one spot, a Coonass will not be far behind. Just to give you an example of some of the ridiculous things we do to spark a party, I will tell you about a *Chatee-Vadee*. The term *Chatee-Vadee* roughly translates into a "pot party" and no, I'm not talking about weed either. A *Chatee-Vadee* is held when a married couple separates and then gets back together. The band of Cajuns gets together and gathers outside of the couple's home either on foot or in vehicles. If in vehicles, the group will drag huge items such as washing machines and wheel barrows. If on foot, they will simply camp in front of the house, banging on pots and pans, hence the term "pot party". The goal is to make so much noise, that the couple comes outside and invites the group in their home to host a meal for them. During one *Chatee-Vadee*, I can remember the empty shell of a Volkswagen Beetle being dragged upside-down on the road, leaving a trail of sparks behind. As I type this; I cannot help but say, "My God, we sound like a bunch of hillbillies." Still, when reminiscing, I can only be saddened, because those are times long gone. People these days are so preoccupied with other things that they lose that piece of heritage, ultimately devolving from their roots. One of my favorite events when growing up was a *boucherie*. A *boucherie*, or butchering, is when a corn-fed pig is butchered. For those of you who don't know, if you give a Coonass a pig, he will ultimately bring you back the hooves and a handful of teeth. Absolutely nothing gets thrown away when butchering a pig. During a *boucherie*, various stations are set up. One group takes the head and proceeds to make hog-head cheese (*fromage da tete de cochon*), which is absolutely revolting to watch when being made, yet taste very good. Another group takes the intestines and begins the lengthy process of making *boudin*, or blood pudding. *Boudin* is simply a mixture of pork meat and rice, stuffed through a portion of the intestine. Pig blood is added, giving it its name. While this is all going on, a third group takes slabs of pig skin and cuts them up in small cubes, frying them in a pot of grease, ultimately making cracklins, also known as *gratons*. Finally, the last group takes the hollowed out shell of the pig and roast it over an open flame. Needless to say, when the day is over, you look like a Jeffery Dahmer victim and your cholesterol is probably up by twenty points, yet you have a full stomach and had a great time with family and friends.

As unconventional as my approach is, in order for you to truly get a look into Louisiana, you must first see the stuff that makes us tick. Besides, I did say that I was going to bring you a different side of paranormal investigating and even though I may not be the smartest man, I can pretty much guarantee that this is the first paranormal-related book in history that talked about running around someone's house while banging pots and pans together with the hopes of getting free food and beer. This, my friends, is Louisiana ghost hunting at its finest.

As I grew older, my interest never changed much. I was not like your average teenager, rambling the roads and chasing girls. Being an only child, I stayed pretty much to myself, which is ironic because I am quite different these days, usually being the first one to take charge of something. When I was around fifteen, I began spending a lot of time with my dad's mother, or as I called her, "Maw-maw". Maw-maw was the sweetest person you could ever meet. Standing about five feet and weighing only about ninety pounds, she still always found a way to sarcastically tell you to go to hell, while smirking the whole time. She had that personality that you could quickly be drawn to. Especially during summer months, I would spend my weekends with her, mowing her lawn to earn some money to buy school clothes. I knew that if I didn't save my own money to buy name brand clothes, which was a necessity in high school, I would be forced to don the garb courtesy of our local "Wally World", which wasn't going to happen. When speaking to maw-maw, she was the type of person that always had interesting stories. Not the usual "I had to walk fifteen miles in the snow to get to school while eating dirt for supper" type stories, but interesting stories that would make you wonder. On many occasions, she would tell me about her husband, who had died when I was only two years old. Her stories were not of when he was living, but tales of strange occurrences after his death. She told me of times where she would be watching television and feel her husband approach her and begin to rub her shoulders. I then began to seriously consider if there was some validity to these claims. If there is a couple who has been married for fifty years, experiencing huge life events together, and one of them dies, who is to say that some part of that long lasting bond cannot stay behind? That is the question that truly began to spark my interest in the paranormal.

As time passed, and I grew older, the bond between my grandmother and I grew stronger and stronger. She would continue telling me accounts of strange experiences she had, as well as those had by other family members. Then one day, when I was seventeen, she told me of a strange occurrence that happened that afternoon. She said that while she was in her chair, a large black mist seemed to appear over her head, literally shrouding her. The mist hovered over her for only a few seconds and then quickly dissipated. She had no clue as to what this could have been, being this had never happened before. The very next day, she went to the doctor for a checkup, only to find out she had liver cancer and was given two months to live. Needless to say, I was devastated. I then began to wonder about what she had previously mentioned about the black mist. Could this have literally been death on her doorstep? After a quick downward spiral and two months to the day that she was diagnosed with cancer, my grandmother passed away. How could the energy from such a wonderful person just fade off into nothing? Where did it go? Where did she go? Is any of that energy remaining? Does she look down on me from heaven? These, along with millions of other questions, raced through my head. To this day, I wonder if maw-maw is looking down on me, proud of what I have become. You will always be missed and loved Maw-maw. Hopefully one day we can meet again so you can look at me with that sarcastic smile, and once again, tell me, "awww … you can just go to hell."

Death is always a hard issue to deal with. By this time, the only grandparent I had left was my mom's father. His wife, "grandma", had died when I was ten and also had her share of strange paranormal stories. Many years before, they had lost a baby girl during childbirth and would occasionally mention her to me. When I was eighteen, my grandfather's health began to deteriorate and he soon became bedridden, passing away soon after. For a week or two prior to his death, he was literally in a coma, not saying a word or even opening his eyes. Then, strangely, on the night before he died, his eyes were wide open, with an almost gleeful look on his face, speaking very coherently. We were all very excited to see him in this condition. As we all huddled around his bed, he then began staring at one corner of the ceiling as he spoke in French to say, "*regardez ma petites fille et epouse,*" which basically translated to "look at my little girl and wife." He then died only a few hours later. I have often heard of cases where people are visited by deceased family members just prior to their own deaths. Could this have been the case with my grandfather? Could his deceased wife and daughter whom died at childbirth been there to take him away appeared? Again, more unanswered questions regarding life after death added to the many I had from the passing of my grandmother.

So there I was, first year in college and no more grandparents. I initially began college with a major in Criminal Justice with the dreams of becoming a Louisiana State Trooper. Those dreams quickly dwindled down to just that: a dream. I found myself being a Sheriff's Deputy for three years then moving on to working for the Federal Bureau of Prisons as a Federal Correctional Officer which, in my opinion, is nothing more than a glorified babysitter, dealing with some of the biggest pieces of manure that God could have unfortunately created. I could go into a day in the life of a HACK (horse's ass carrying keys), but that could be a book all in itself. Prisons are some of the best breeding grounds for possible hauntings. For example, Angola State Penitentiary in Angola, Louisiana, is said to be one of the bloodiest, and oldest, prisons in America. For years, I have heard stories from former employees claiming of haunted activity coming from some of the older buildings such as the old "death house" and women's dormitory. If you think about it, prisons are home to some of the most negative energy around, radiating from some of the most negative people, many of which have committed crimes in these prisons such as murder and rape. Other incidents, such as severe assaults and suicide, only add to the possibilities of hauntings.

At the time, I had been employed with the Bureau for about three years, putting the age of the institution at only four. Although the facility was extremely new, it had already had a few unnatural deaths, if you know what I mean. I was working the graveyard shift, which consists of midnight until eight in the morning. I was assigned to a housing unit of approximately 128 inmates, all of which were secured in their cells. Needless to say, there isn't much to do in a dark housing unit at two in the morning with no one to talk to, so you often resort to reading, surfing the web, and even taking a power nap. I always found it hard to sleep because you never really knew who could sneak up on you and the chairs were way too uncomfortable. What I would often do, is prop my feet on the desk and lean back, basically to just chill out. During this shift, we often had a Lieutenant who was notorious for sneaking in the unit from upstairs, in an attempt to catch the officer sleeping. It was for this additional reason that I never slept. The unit I was working at this time was actually the home to a suicide a few months before. I had heard from a few of the officers that previously worked the unit that they would hear and see strange things during the graveyard shift. Little did I know that I would soon be one of those officers. It started on one particular night at around two in the morning. I had assumed the position: feet on desk and kicked back, when I heard the sound of footsteps coming down the stairs. They were quite loud, as if the person was forcefully descending the stairs. I immediately assumed that it was the Lieutenant, holding his keys, trying to sneak in the unit. I slowly sat up and made my way to the stairs, only to find that no one was there. This went on for several weeks, as I would get up to try and find the source of the footsteps, only to find nothing but 128 snoring and flatulence-filled "rightfully convicted felons." On one occasion, around 2:00 AM again, I was reading through the inmates' outgoing mail, which is the main duty for the morning watch shift. As I was reading, in the corner of my eye, I saw, what appeared to be a male wearing a white t-shirt, walking across the unit floor. As mentioned, during these hours, all inmates are secured in their cells so I quickly made a round to check if I had any doors that were unsecured. All sixty-four cells were locked. A few weeks went by, as I would continue hearing the footsteps and occasionally seeing this figure in the corner of my eye. Not yet having my "investigating eye", I would often blow the incidents off as being tired. It wasn't until I spoke with the officers who had experiences in that unit did I realized that our stories matched perfectly. We all heard the same phantom footsteps and witnessed the figure with the white t-shirt. On several occasions, I even had some of the inmates assigned to that unit approach me and tell me they had seen a person walking in front of their cells during times that I wasn't making any rounds.

With all the unanswered questions I had from the deaths of my grandparents and now the strange events that I experienced while at work, I had to take the next step. I had to start educating myself in this fascinating field. I began reading tons of books on places across Louisiana that were said to be haunted and even began to visit a few. What better place to start my paranormal search than the "Big Easy" itself, New Orleans. For some strange reason, New Orleans has always been very close to my heart. I often jokingly say that I must have been a New Orleans resident in a former life. For those of you who have never been to New Orleans, it truly is a unique city, different from any other one I have ever been to. Settled in 1718, New Orleans was basically a dumping ground for the worst of society from other areas. Rapists, murderers, and thieves, were literally banished to New Orleans, which was already a tense melting pot of cultures, such as the Spanish, Irish, and French. What resulted from this mixture was a tremendous increase in crime and murder. To this day, you can stroll through the French Quarters and find that just about every building there has some sort of gruesome tale from years before. Many groups often claim that their state is the most active due to major

Civil War battles. I can honestly say, with a straight face, that I truly feel New Orleans to be in the top three.

On my first few visits to New Orleans, I simply walked around, absorbing the immense culture abound. Only in New Orleans can you be distracted from admiring the beautiful two hundred fifty year old architecture, by a guy passing, wearing only leather chaps and a pink boa. The sad thing is that when he does pass, no one really even gives him a second look. As I walked the Quarter, I began to see numerous fliers for "Ghost Tours" that advertised a guided nighttime tour through the French Quarter, introducing you to its "gruesome past". I quickly cut out my two dollar coupon and rushed to one of the many voodoo shops, which was the starting point for the tour. What I found was a group of eager tourists standing at attention in front of some guy that looked like a total freak. He was standing there with a cheap black cape, a black top hat, and spoke with the cheesiest Transylvanian accent you could ever imagine. I then realized why the tour was only eight dollars, with my coupon of course. To my surprise, despite the terrible theatrics courtesy of "Generic Dracula", we were actually taken to some very interesting homes that contained some fascinating history. Places such as the Bottom of the Cup Tea Room, where a young prostitute froze to death on the roof as a sign of devotion to her lover, and the private residence that was once home to a mad butcher who used his wife as one of the "secret ingredients" in his meat were just a few of the locations that pulled me deeper and deeper into the atmosphere of haunted New Orleans. Still, of all the locations I was introduced to during my tour, no building struck as much interest as the LaLaurie Mansion, located on 1140 Royal St.

The LaLaurie Mansion is a massive, three-story home that nearly takes up an entire street block. The mansion received its name from its infamous owners, Dr. Louis LaLaurie and Madame Marie Delphine LaLaurie. The two were very wealthy and held a high status amongst society. Madame LaLaurie however, is most known for her torturous treatment of her servants. In one reported case, a young servant was brushing Madame LaLaurie's hair and accidentally snagged one of her locks. After an outburst from Madame LaLaurie, who was also known for cowhiding her servants, the young girl fled from the room and onto the rooftop, where she accidentally fell to her death. Reports from neighbors said that the body of the young girl was then collected and buried in a well on the property. April 10, 1834 would go down in the record books as one of the most infamous days in New Orleans history. According to records, a fire broke out in the adjacent cookhouse. Responding firefighters found that the fire had been intentionally set by two servants that were chained to the stove. The fire was apparently set to get the attention of others. The worst was still yet to come, as the firefighters made their way to the attic. What they found in that crawlspace could never truly be described in mere words. They found over a dozen slaves that were tortured and subjected to horrible medical experiments. According to reports, one woman was disemboweled, having her entrails nailed to the floor. Others had their limbs broken and reset in strange positions to appear like crabs. One young boy had all the skin removed from his face, exposing veins, bones, and muscle. Some had been literally impaled to the wall, had fecal matter shoved in their mouths, and then sewn shut. Finally, one poor soul, who had been dead for quite some time, had a stick protruding from his skull, which was used to apparently stir his brains. The horrified mob that gathered outside became enraged, now seeking retaliation on the LaLauries. Unfortunately, before the mob could get their hands on the two, they bolted from the scene via a horse and carriage. It is unclear as to whatever happened to the couple. Some say that Madame LaLaurie lived the remainder of her days on the north shore of Lake Ponchatrain. Most people concur that Lalaurie died on December 7, 1842, and her body secretly returned to New Orleans. In the early 1900's, Eugene Backes, who served as sexton to St. Louis Cemetery #1 until 1924, discovered an old cracked, copper plate in Alley 4 of St. Louis cemetery. The inscription on the plate read: *"Madame Lalaurie, Marie Delphine Macarty, decede a Paris, le 7 Decembre, 1842, a l'age De 6-"*

It is that very type of morbid, yet intriguing, history that ultimately set me on a determined course to investigate buildings similar to the LaLaurie Mansion. The questioned remained: "How in the hell would I get started?" I knew I couldn't just show up on the doorsteps of some of these historical locations and say, "Hey, can I spend the night in here and look for ghosts?" In order for me to become established enough to get to that point, I would have to crawl before I walked. I then made my way back home knowing I had to basically start where every other "ghost hunter-in-training" started: My local cemeteries. The question then became: "What cemetery would be a good place to visit?" It is at this time, my good friend, Jason, introduced me to a little cemetery known as Ft. Derussy. Little did I know that this was the start of an adventurous journey.

2

FT. DERUSSY CEMETERY (MARKSVILLE, LA)

Deep in the backwoods of Marksville, Louisiana, lays Ft. Derussy Battlefield. The fort that was founded on this field received its name from Colonel Louis G. Derussy, commander of the 2nd Louisiana Regiment of volunteers during the Civil

War. Colonel Derussy's primary goal was to build a defense along the Red River in an attempt to stop the Union army, who were approaching from Simmesport via the Atchafalaya River.

In May of 1863, Federal boats approached a near underwater Fort Derussy, destroying several of its cannons. The fort was only partially demolished, as the Union soldiers ran out of gun powder. The Confederacy soon returned and made repairs to the damaged fort. A year later, on May 14, 1864, the Union returned, now led by Colonel William F. Lynch and Colonel William T. Shaw, invoking a battle between both sides. Only two hours had passed, yet the Confederacy had surrendered, leaving five soldiers dead and four wounded. In total, 317 Confederate soldiers were taken prisoner, twenty-nine of them being officers. The Union then began to completely demolish the fort, using explosives to dismantle the sturdy base. During this process, it is said that three soldiers accidentally died, when an explosive literally blew their heads off. Nowadays, all that is left of the fort is a large dirt mound covered with trees and large brush.

On the outskirts of the actual battlefield, lays the Ft. Derussy Cemetery. Growing up, I was never even aware of its existence. It wasn't until I was around twenty-one, did I hear of the place. First, I must mention one of my best friends, Jason Ponthieux. Jason is one of the coolest, most laid back people you could ever meet. I first met Jason when I worked for the Sheriff's Department. We were literally partners in crime, always together, being sure to close down the local bar every Saturday night. On one of our many forays into the bars, one of us brought up the topic of the paranormal. I then remember Jason saying, "Did you ever hear of Ft. Derussy Cemetery?" After telling him no, he went on to say that it was the creepiest cemetery he had ever been to, guaranteeing that there had to be something paranormal there. He went on to tell me that the cemetery had long been a hangout spot for local teenagers, basically wanting the hell scared out of them. They would arrive in packs to search for the grave of a reported "witch", said to be buried there. No one could ever give a straight answer as to who this "witch" was and where she was buried. Some say she was buried on the outside of the small picket fence, due to the non-consecrated soil. Others would simply camp out on any given grave with a Ouija board and goof off.

When Jason first told me the strange stories connected to the fort, they simply seemed like high school urban legends. It was then, that Jason told me of an incident involving a friend of ours. One of the high school legends was that if you would park your vehicle in the cul de sac, which is basically a large circle, and shut off your engine, you would be able to hear strange noises. On this particular night, our friend, who was never known to exaggerate or tell lies, brought his girlfriend and their friend to the cemetery to test this theory out. They entered the cemetery and parked their vehicle in the center of the large, circled entrance, shutting off the engine. They nervously say there in the quiet cemetery, waiting for something to happen. Minutes passed and nothing happened, only affirming the idea that these rumors were probably just a load of crap, told to scare kids. Just when the three were getting ready to leave, they began to hear what sounding like scratching along the side of my friend's extended cab truck. The scratching sounded almost like someone running a stick alongside the vehicle. Needless to say, this was all it took for the three to decide it was time to get the hell out of Dodge. As my friend attempted to start his truck, which was only months old, the damn thing would not start. His girlfriend then began to scream, saying that it felt like someone was trying to choke her. As more attempts to start the vehicle failed, the third person, who was sitting in the backseat, looked towards the rear of the truck and claimed seeing a "small black creature, approximately three to four feet tall, trying to climb in the back of the truck." By this time, I can only imagine that the three were literally terrified. Moments later, the vehicle started up and the three left Ft. Derussy Cemetery, never to return again.

Let me be the first to say that when I initially heard the story, I immediately blew it off as a load of crap. Jason then quickly informed me that after hearing the story from our friend, he then questioned the individual who was sitting in the back seat of the truck that night, not knowing that Jason already heard one version of the story. What was then told to Jason by the third party was the exact same story that was originally told, matching word for word. Could there have been some truth to this outlandish story? I then began to focus on the claims regarding the small black "creature" that was seen at the rear of the truck. What the hell could that have been? It wasn't until about four years later, while speaking to an individual very educated in the paranormal, that I was told about a "Devil's Run". According to this individual, a Devil's Run is "a small creature, approximately three to four feet tall, with no facial features, which is said to hang out in or near cemeteries. They are not spirits, but actual beings, that can be killed. Despite their small stature, they are very dense creatures, weighing in excess of three hundred pounds. They primarily tend to focus their threats on pregnant women." Trust me, you're not the only one scratching your head on this one. When I first heard that, I found it very hard to believe myself. What I then did was take this newly found knowledge and began to question Jason again on the incident. The first question I asked was, "Was either of the two girls pregnant that night?" To my surprise, after some thought, Jason did recall that the girlfriend of our friend was, in fact, pregnant at the time this took place. Please keep in mind that this was the same person that reported to have felt being choked as they attempted to depart the cemetery. I then began to ponder the questions: When does coincidence become more than that? At what point do reoccurring events at particular times mean more than simple chance? If it isn't chance, then what is it? Again, more questions added to the million and one I already had. Returning to the night I was first told about the cemetery; what happened next was inevitable: Jason then asked, "Hey, do you want to go see where the cemetery is at?"

It was going on three in the morning and we were now making our way to the cemetery. Needless to say, I was a little nervous, yet I had plenty "liquid courage" still left in my system from the night's festivities. We then began to drive a little out of the city limits, turning off of highway 107, and towards the battlefield. As we drove, Jason went into his "commentator mode", explaining how creepy the place was, reminding me of that damn little black creature, running around peoples' trucks. He then continued to set the mood by making little snide remarks such as, "You just wait until we pull up and you see that creepy road." Keep in mind that this was still all so new to me and I didn't quite have the courage that I would have later on when I would really be getting serious in the paranormal. I will be the first to admit that his remarks were taking their toll on me, as we approached the infamous road that he kept mentioning. As we crossed over a small bridge, there appeared a very crudely-made sign on the side of the road that said, "Ft. Derussy Cemetery 1862." Next to the sign was a small, gravel road that led into wooded area. "You have got to be shitting me." was all I could say to Jason. All he could do was let out this wicked little laugh, symbolically saying, "I told you so." We turned onto the small road, which was just wide enough to fit one vehicle. There was no turning back now, as the only way to get out was to go all the way to the end of the road, where it opened up to the cemetery, and then turn around. I swear, this had to be one of the darkest and most secluded roads I have ever been on. Time felt like it was frozen, as every time we would near a curve, expecting to see the cemetery, it would just be another long stretch. My unsettling nerves were quickly growing, as all I could hear was the gravel crunching under the tires and the branches scraping alongside the truck. What made it worse while we were driving was that I could not stop looking behind me, in the back of Jason's truck, literally picturing a small black creature running laps around the bed of the truck. By this time, my nerves had completely banished any residue of alcohol in my system, as I was now sober as a priest on Sunday morning. (Side note: If you are ever drunk and need to sober up quick, go get the hell scared out of you.) Just when I thought there was no end in sight, the trees finally parted like the Red Sea, exposing this very small cemetery, surrounded by a small picket fence. To this day, I don't know if it was first time jitters or what, but I got a massive surge of fear that rushed through me. I didn't know what it was or what was causing it, but I knew I just needed to get away from that place. All I can remember from that night was not even getting out the truck and repeatedly yelling, "Turn around. Turn around. Turn the hell around." Jason, now overcome with laughter, circled the cul de sac, and left the cemetery. So much for a brave ghost hunter, as my first visit to the infamous Ft. Derussy cemetery was a complete flop.

As expected, my "brave" antics were the butt of many jokes for quite some time. Jason would often sarcastically ask, "Hey man, wanna go to Ft. Derussy again?" Still, despite the fear I had that night, something was still drawing me not only to the cemetery, but to any and all locations said to be haunted. About a year or so would pass with no mention of returning to the cemetery. However, during this time, I continued to extensively research locations throughout the state, along with the basic how-to's of paranormal investigating. During this research period, I would often come across mentions of Ft. Derussy. An interesting book, written in the early 1940's, vaguely refers to the area as, "the haunted woods near Marksville where the local people refuse to go after dark." Still, regardless of what information was being found, one thing was certain: I had to muster the courage to make a return visit to the cemetery. Maybe this time, I could at least be brave enough to get out of the vehicle.

For my second visit, I would definitely need some back up. I would look no further than good old Jason for that moral support. I would also be bringing my friend, Dustyn, who I also worked with at the prison and later found out had a huge interest in the paranormal as well. Together, the three of us would attempt to re-visit the cemetery under the cover of darkness, not only to possibly have a ghostly encounter, but to try and redeem myself after my initial pathetic attempt. As we drove, we were telling Dustyn the whole story about our friend's encounter with the black creature, which quickly rekindled an oh-so-familiar nervousness in me. Still, I was determined to face my demons (no pun intended) and finally visit the cemetery at night. The three of us arrived at the cemetery with the very basic in equipment: One flashlight for three people. The flashlight we had was a standard re-chargeable MagLite, which had been fully charged prior to our visit. For those of you not familiar with rechargeable flashlights, they usually give off several hours of continuous burn time when fully charged.

We pulled into the entrance of the cemetery, which is simply a large grass circle. We reached the small picket fence outlining the cemetery, which is no bigger than an acre or so. Above the entrance was a large wooden sign that resembled the one at the road which said, "Ft. Derussy Cemetery 1862." I can remember it being an extremely dark night, with not a bit of moonlight breaking through the cloud-filled sky. It was reaching the summer months, which in Louisiana, means one thing: mosquitoes, mosquitoes, mosquitoes, and more mosquitoes. We slowly crossed the picket gate, clinching on to our flashlights as if they were samurai swords. Immediately upon entering, I noticed a grave to my left that was ornately decorated with flowers, pictures, trinkets, and a strange little star. What made this star so creepy was that it had a solar light on it and at night it would give off this weird blue glow, only adding to the creep factor. To my right, was an extremely old grave that was enclosed by a rusty wrought-iron fence. Behind that grave was a tree that had one of its limbs cut off. On this stump, someone had drawn the silhouette of a man resembling Jesus in charcoal. We continued to trek towards the rear of the cemetery, where we noticed an area that was roped off. In this area, there were no visible graves. All that was there were grass, loose bricks, and a sign which read:

> "NOTICE: No burial beyond this point because of the unmarked graves of Civil War soldiers."

At this time, I began shining my flashlight into the tree line, which was actually the backside of what was left of the original fort. As I panned back and forth, I could have sworn that I had seen a figure dodge behind one of the trees. It could have simply been a shadowed effect caused by the moving light and the tree limbs, yet it was more than enough for me to turn to Jason and say, "Alright man, I think it's time to get going." As the three of us made our way back to the entrance, we stopped at the center of the cemetery, which consisted of three large cypress trees and a fenced in area containing three graves. It wasn't until later that we learned that the graves belonged to a father, mother, and teenage daughter. The father had, in fact, murdered his wife and daughter, and then committed suicide. Surprisingly, after this horrible event, they were still all buried side by side, which I never quite understood. As we paused for a moment, I turned to Dustyn, who was holding the flashlight, only to see that this flashlight that had been shining bright the entire time was quickly draining down to a dull orange glow. At the exact same time, the three of us all felt this massive rush come over us, basically telling us to, "get the hell out." We all looked at each other, knowing what we were each thinking. The three of us literally locked arms as we shuffled our way back to the entrance, using the faint glow of the flashlight to light our way back. As we made our way through the gate and onto the other side of the cemetery, the flashlight instantly returned to its fully lit state. To this day, I have never witnessed such an impressive form of energy drain as I did that night. About a year later, as part of an established group, I would take a camera crew from California to the cemetery to do some filming. As we were in the exact same spot, I explained to the crew about our incident with the flashlight, when all of a sudden, all three video cameras that the crew was using died in unison. As I said, how unique does the coincidence have to be before it is acknowledged as being more than that?

That particular night with the drained flashlight stayed in my mind for quite some time. It would be a while before I would return to Ft. Derussy due to the fact that we were approaching the summer months. You may ask, "Why the summer months?" I might as well tell you now, yet I will mention it many more times throughout the book, but I suffer from severe arachnophobia. Since I was a child,

I have been absolutely terrified of spiders and everything that they stand for. I will literally scream like a freaking girl if I so much as think that one may be on me. Ft. Derussy is a prime breeding ground for spiders during the summer months, and not just any spiders, but those disgusting looking banana spiders that make the huge webs with the "zig zag" design in the center. I swear to you, as I type this, I am already getting goose bumps just thinking of those damn critters.

With the summertime here, I retreated to my nice, spider-free abode, to continue my research on locations throughout the state. I had found a very informative site that was dedicated to the preservation of the Ft. Derussy Battlefield. After hesitantly contacting some of the members of the preservation society, I was fortunate enough to receive a response from one of their very knowledgeable members. During our correspondences, I learned some very interesting things about the actual fort, battlefield, and cemetery, including the legends regarding the infamous "witch" said to have been buried on the grounds. Below is an actual excerpt from one of our first conversations:

> "Local high-school kids frequently go out to the cemetery, and it has a reputation of being quite a scary place to be. I was at a car repair shop once, and one of the mechanics told me he would never go out there again, as the last time he went the gate had closed on its own behind them, and he and his friends had heard screaming from the direction of the fort. They'd left in a hurry, and never been back. He said he wouldn't even go out there in the daytime, and suggested that I not go out there either.
>
> The picket fence around the cemetery is new (2000). It now encloses a grave that used to be outside the old fence. There is a story about why that grave was outside the fence, but I've never been able to get a straight story as to exactly why that was. Some say it was a suicide, others say it was a white man who had married a colored woman, and others refuse to talk about it.
>
> The oldest marked grave is from the late 1890s. The cemetery was used at least as early as 1862, and has a large number of old unmarked graves. It is still in use, but it is doubtful whether there is anywhere you can dig a grave in the cemetery that isn't on top of an old grave."

One thing about legends: There are always different versions of the story. The same is the case with the Ft. Derussy witch. Some say it is simply a white male who was married to a black woman, others say it was a white male married to a woman who practiced the black arts, while others say it was simply a witch. Whatever the case may be, there has been plenty of people fascinated in the legend. Most recently, I received an e-mail about a month ago from an anonymous sender, referencing to the "witch". Her letter was as follows:

> "My sister and I went to the cemetery before the new fence was put up and the "witch" was still buried outside of the cemetery. At that time you could barely make out her first name, Valeree, but not her last. My older sister's curiosity about her led to finding another young woman in the area and this woman said she researched and found more information. According to her, the witches name was Valeree Redfield, and she lived in Shreveport. If memory serves me correctly, Redfield was her married name and she was murdered under suspicious circumstances in Shreveport. She was brought to Ft. Derussy for burial because she was a Marksville native and buried

outside the cemetery because her people thought she was into the Black Arts and witchcraft."

So see, legends come in all different shapes and sizes. Some are legitimate; some are stretched to make for good campfire stories, while others are plain old crocks of crapolla. Whatever the case may be, one thing will always be certain: They make up a wonderful part of Louisiana folklore.

3
LOUISIANA FOLKLORE

There has always been something intriguing to me about Louisiana folklore. When growing up, my parents never threatened me with the traditional "boogey man" or monster under my bed. It was always strange, imaginary individuals such as "Johnny Panachaffa", the old homeless man that lived in the woods, who would enter the bedrooms of misbehaving children and "pull their toes." I never quite understood the whole "pulling your toes" concept. Of all the things that a "boogey man" could do, why pull your toes? Old Johnny was a universal threat for anything that you did that you weren't supposed to do. Didn't go to sleep; I'm calling Johnny Panachaffa. Don't keep still; I'm calling Johnny Panachaffa. Growing up, I never quite understood how my parents could call a man who was supposed to be homeless and lived in the woods.? Looking back, I find the whole idea amusing, yet growing up, it sure was a quick way to instill terror in the eyes of Cajun children everywhere. To this day, I find myself doing the same thing with my daughter. She is terrified of a certain horror show where "killer slugs" infest peoples' brains. When she starts acting up, all I have to say is "Don't make me call the slugs." Those simple words are all it takes to send my child running for the hills in tears. The same applies to much of Louisiana legend and folklore, except it applies to adults as well. When I mention Louisiana Folklore to people who aren't from the state, one of the first things they think of is Voodoo.

Voodoo originated from the West African Yoruba people who lived in 18th and 19th century Dahomey. Slaves brought their religion with them when they were forcibly shipped to Haiti and other islands in the West Indies. Hoodoo refers to

African traditional folk magic. A rich magical tradition which was (for thousands of years), indigenous to ancient African botanical, magio-religious practices and folk cultures, its practice was imported when mainly West Africans were enslaved and brought to the United States. As this practice seemed too taboo, slaves were obviously banned from practicing this religion, so they looked for ways to covertly use it. This is why much of Voodoo is heavily influenced by French and Spanish Catholicism. Many of the Voodoo *Lwa*, or Gods, are symbolized by Catholic Saints such as St. Peter, St. Michael, and St. Christopher.

When people initially hear the word "Voodoo" they quickly envision people flopping around on the floor, ringing chickens' necks, while drinking goats' blood. Sure, in some areas, this does actually take place, but there are many facets of Voodoo that are quite tame. The same applies to other practices such as Witchcraft, where there is "white magic" and "black magic". Many Voodoo practitioners simply incorporate the religion into their daily life by praying to a desired deity, or *Lwa*, in the hopes of accomplishing a specific task. For example, if one were to pray for money or wealth, they would direct their prayer towards *Papa Legba*. *Papa Legba* is the intermediary between the *Lwa* and humanity. He stands at a spiritual crossroads and gives (or denies) permission to speak with the spirits and translates between the human and "angelic" and all other languages. If someone were to "work" a dark spell, such as crossing or hexing, they would focus their prayer towards *Baron Samedi*. *Baron Samedi* is known as the "*Lwa* of the dead" and is usually depicted with a white top hat, black tuxedo, dark glasses, and cotton plugs in the nostrils, as if to resemble a corpse dressed and prepared for burial in Haitian style. *Baron Samedi* stands at the crossroads, where the souls of dead humans pass on their way to Guinee. As well as being the all-knowing *Lwa* of death, he is a sexual *Lwa*, frequently represented by phallic symbols and noted for disruption, obscenity, debauchery, and having a particular fondness for tobacco and rum.

For those who practice Voodoo, for whatever reasons, the number one thing is that they have to believe for it to work. Voodoo, as with all religions, is based on a matter of faith. The use of herbs, candles, and amulets are merely a catalyst for whatever task you are attempting to accomplish. The power lies in the faith of the practitioner. For any practitioner, one of the first things an individual does is set up his or her altar. The altar is set up in a quiet area, away from all distractions. It simply consists of a small table, covered in a layer of cloth. The color of cloth depends on the type of spell you are working: Love (red), luck or money (green), hexing (black), and protection (white). In the center of the altar, an incense burner is often place, burning a specific incense to match the spell. For example, Dragon's Blood or Nag Champa would be used in a protection spell. Accompanying the incense is normally a burning candle. Its color, as with the cloth, correlates to whichever ritual is being conducted. At the rear of the altar, you would then place offerings to the *Lwa*, such as fresh flowers, hard candies, alcohol, and a *veve*. A *veve* is a religious symbol that serves as a representation for the *Lwa* during rituals. Every *Lwa* has their own *veve* and is usually drawn on the floor by strewing a powder-like substance, such as cornmeal, wheat flour, bark, red brick powder, or gunpowder. At the rear of the altar, one would often find an "earth" offering, which is normally salt, a container of holy water, voodoo doll, and "mojo bag". The voodoo doll and mojo bag, sometimes called a conjure bag, must also match the color of the ritual you are working. The mojo bag usually contains a mixture of herbs, powders, personal concerns, such as hair or fingernail clippings, coins, lodestones, a petition paper or prayer, and other objects thought to promote supernatural action or protection. The tying of the bag is an important part of its making, as this keeps within it the spirit whose aid is being sought. Once fixed and prepared, the mojo is *fed* to keep it working, generally with a liquid, such as a perfume, anointing oil, or in some cases a drop of urine.

With the altar complete, the practitioner will then begin by cleansing the area with holy water. He/she will then sit and begin to meditate in attempts of expelling all other thoughts in their mind, while often reciting prayers from the Book of Psalms. The practitioner will then light the incense and candle, "bathing" the mojo bag and voodoo doll in the smoke. The purpose of the mojo bag is to basically serve as a portable altar device, possessing all the characteristics of the ritual performed. By carrying the bag on you at all times, normally on your strong side, you are reminded of the ritual. It is said that the more you "work", or knead, the bag, the more energy it will release. Next, a message referring to the desired ritual is then written on parchment paper, affixed to the back of the doll. Even the type of ink used often relates to the type of spell he or she is working with. For example, "pigeon's blood" ink would be used for a love spell and "bat's blood" ink would be used for a hexing spell.

Although I do not practice Voodoo, I find the practice absolutely fascinating, so I constantly read up on the subject. Besides, I am way too chicken to even try some of these spells. If it wasn't for bad luck, I wouldn't have any at all, so for me to even try and tempt faith by challenging karma would simply be asinine on my part. I simply wanted to give you as in-depth of a look that I could into one of the more mysterious portions of Louisiana folklore.

Cryptozoology, which is the search for animals that fall outside of the known zoological categories, is another fascinating field of study. Often looked at as a farce, the study of this field has yielded the discovery of actual creatures such as the giant squid, Komodo dragon, and the platypus. So is the case with much of science, as anything new often draws mockery. It is only with time, and scientific analysis, that legitimate findings are discovered, shutting up all those who were too close minded to initially grasp the idea.

No matter what portion of the country you live in, there are tales of some unknown creature that lurks in the shadows of the surrounding area. If you live in the northeast portion of the country, tales of the Mothman are often told, whereas stories of Bigfoot are abound in the west. Other cryptids regularly searched for are the Loch Ness Monster, Jersey Devil, Yeti, and Chupacabra. One lesser-known cryptid, said to inhabit the southern portion of Louisiana is the *Loup Garou*.

The *Loup Garou*, which means French Werewolf, has long rumored to terrorize the Cajuns of southern Louisiana. In the Cajun legend, the creature is said to prowl the swamps around Acadiana and greater New Orleans, and possibly the fields or forests of the regions. The *Loup Garou* most often is noted as a creature with a human body and the head of a wolf or dog, similar to the werewolf legend. Often, the story-telling was used for fear. One example is that stories were told by elders to persuade Cajun children to behave. Another example relates that the wolf-like beast will hunt down and kill Catholics who do not follow the rules of Lent. A common blood sucking legend speculated that the *Loup Garou* was under the spell for 101 days. After that time, the curse was transferred from person to person when the *Loup Garou* drew another human's blood. During the day the creature returned to human form. Although acting sickly, the human refrained to tell others of the situation for fear of being killed. It is also said in legend that the *Loup Garou* simply originates from lycanthropy, or the ability for a human to transform into wolf-like characteristics.

Another creature said to inhabit the backwoods of Louisiana is the Honey Island Swamp Monster. Honey Island is a massive 70,000-acre swamp in Pearl River. In it, there is said to live a bipedal creature, standing approximately seven feet tall with gray hair and yellow eyes. A local legend tells of a train crash in the area in the early twentieth century. A traveling circus was on the train and from it a group of chimpanzees, and interbred with the local alligator population. The first reported sighting was in 1963, when an inspiring photographer, Harlan Ford, claimed to have obtained photographic proof of the creature, along with several cast moldings of its footprints.

Other than crytozoological creatures, there are said to be other strange occurrences found in "Cajun Country". One of these that have always intrigued me was the *Fee Fo Lais*. Also called *Feaux Follets* and "Will O' Wisps", these mysterious lights of unknown origin are said to be the damned spirits of criminals or Catholics who served under Satan. The name roughly translates to "Merry Fires" or "Fire Flowers". As a child, I often recalled my grandmother and mother talk about these lights. According to them, if you would see one of these strange lights, it was an omen that something bad was going to happen. When describing the lights, they simply said they looked like glowing balls of orange light, about the size of a volleyball, which could be seen literally bouncing across fields, most commonly near cemeteries. According to my grandmother, they were also often seen following fence lines. In order to get rid of one, you had to place a needle on top of one of the fence posts, allowing the *Feaux Follets* to past through the eye of it. Initially, I truly felt that Alzheimers had officially peeked its ugly head on my grandmother's doorstep. However, this was the same woman that once told me to get rid of a wart, I would have to get someone to cut a potato in half and rub it on the wart. They then would have to take the potato and bury it where water would drain off of a building. Days later, the wart was supposed to fall off. Sounds like a load of crap to you? I thought so too, until the day came that I got a wart. Here comes my dad with a half of a potato, rubbing it on the wart. He then went and buried it in an undisclosed location. Call it coincidence, but two days later the damn wart fell off. So you see, it's like they say, "There is a thin line between genius and insanity." Looking back, I sometimes wonder if my grandmother might have known a little bit of "mojo" when it came to home remedies such as the infamous wart remover.

Unlike the potato incident, the *Feaux Follets* were still a tale I was uncertain about. Through the years, I would hear many people talking about these lights, while also hearing many debunk them as labeling the anomalies as swamp gas. Swamp gas is a scientific phenomena caused from flammable gases, such as methane, that are emitted from waterlogged soils and the breakdown of fats, cellulose, and proteins by bacteria found in the mud and sediment of the marsh floor. The result is that these gases are ignited, releasing a light blue or yellow flame. The question is: How are these gases ignited? Tests have been conducted to find the presence of self-igniting gases in the swamps, yet all tests have come back inconclusive.

I would continue to question the validity of these lights until one winter evening in 2005. I was on my way to Lafayette via Hwy 29 in Bunkie, which is a road pretty much running through open fields. It was about 5:00 PM. and the sun was setting. It wasn't completely dark, but enough that I used my headlights for oncoming traffic. As I was approaching a curve, about three hundred to four hundred yards ahead of me, I saw this golden ball of light, which looked like the headlight of a vehicle, emerge from the right side of the road and begin to cross. Initially, I thought it was the headlight from a motorcycle coming my way. While the light was still in the middle of the road, another vehicle came around the corner and was heading in my direction. It was at this point that I could see that the light was not from a vehicle, as there was another car coming and I could see those headlights as well. The strange light then continued to literally float on to the other side of the road and faded into the overgrown weeds. By this time, I was approximately one hundred yards from the initial sighting, and was now certain that what I saw was not the headlight of a motorcycle. As I crossed the sight, and the oncoming car passed me, I came to a complete stop to look in the field where the light floated to. I could not see any lights nor smoke from a possible fire. The damn thing literally vanished. As I began to roll off, I looked to my right and there, to my surprise, was a small cemetery. I then thought back to the stories told to me by my grandmother and what she said about these strange *Feaux Follets* being primarily seen near cemeteries. The pieces of what once seemed to be nothing more than a tell-tale puzzle began to make more and more sense to me. Reports of strange happenings dating back for a hundred or more years must, in my mind, have to have some sort of validity to them.

In addition to these strange tales of stinky wolf men living in swamps and balls of fire, comes even stranger superstitions and colloquialisms. Growing up, my grandmother would always come up with the strangest superstitions. For example, if you were doing the dishes and you dropped the *lavette*, or dish rag, on the floor, you would have company to come over and visit, or *lavais*. If you were to dream of a baby being born, than it meant that someone in the family would be dying soon. However, if you dreamt of someone dying, then a family member was going to become pregnant. If a pregnant woman had hiccups often, the baby would be born with lots of hair. Tickled a baby too much would cause them to stutter once they began to talk. Seeing it rain while the sun was shining was a sign that the devil was beating his wife. Finally, my personal favorite, if you break a mirror, throw the pieces into a stream of running water to "wash away the bad luck."

These were just a small list of some of the strange superstitions told to young children growing up in a Cajun household. In most cases, as with any superstitions, none of them ever really meant anything and rarely even occurred. However, every once and a while these superstitions did come to life, causing us to wonder if there was some truth to any of the crazy tales told to us. It all boils down to a matter of faith and whether or not you are a "glass is half full or half empty" type of person. From a skeptical point of view, the occurring events were merely an example of coincidence. For example, drop the dishrag enough times and eventually someone will visit on the same day. Hardcore believers out there would take that one time, disregarding the tons of other times where they dropped the dishrag and nothing happened, and put even more faith behind the strange superstition.

Returning to the topic of voodoo; for years, there were tales of people rising from the dead and returning as zombies. They were seen wandering around their towns in an altered state, not knowing who they were. The true believers refused to look for any other logical explanations. It took scientists to come in and investigate the occurrences, only to find that the people were not actually zombies that rose from the dead. They were, in fact, given a poison derived from the puffer fish. The concoction was made from the poison tetrodotoxin, one of the deadliest neurotoxins known to man, found in the ovaries and liver of the fish. In very slight doses, the side effects are paralysis, numbness, and loss of memory; all of which are the same characteristics of the "Voodoo zombies."

So you see, lore and legends actually do often exist. However, in many cases, the events do have a scientific explanation. Yet, like with the *Feaux Follets*, there are times when science cannot help, leaving you wondering what else could be out there. This concept would prove to be essential in regards to paranormal investigating. There are so many people out there who are close-minded believers, thinking that every bump in the night is a ghost while, at the same time, there are those who refuse to believe anything can be paranormal and there is a logical explanation for everything, even though they don't know what it is. I would take a little bit from both sides later on when I would become an investigator. The skeptic in me would always stop and try to find a logical explanation for the strange occurrence, while there was still the part in me that knew that some things could not be explained and I would have to take the paranormal into consideration. Even my study in Voodoo would later play a part in investigating, as I would sometimes come across strange trinkets and offerings in cemeteries, allowing me to better understand the situation at hand.

With the vast amount of paranormal groups that seem to pop up on a daily basis, many of them do not realize all that is involved. To be truly knowledgeable in all facets of the field, they must also study other areas such as different religious practices, cemetery iconography, cryptozoology, parapsychology, modern electronics, and, in most cases, simple science. Still, when the smoke clears, I can't help but remember my roots and those good old superstitions told to me as a child. I now know that I have the analytical abilities to recognize and validate an occurrence as a logically-explainable event, yet am open-minded enough to realize that there are things out there that we cannot explain. I think it would be best to wrap up this chapter with the following quote:

"Seeing is believing, yet you have to believe to see."

4

GHOST HUNTING 101

Before I get into the whole "How I became a paranormal investigator" portion of the book, I think now would be the best time to give a somewhat detailed "Ghost Hunting 101" lesson. This way, you can become familiar with some of the terminology and equipment that we use. Hopefully, if I do my job correctly, you will also get an understanding of what to look for, how to obtain quality evidence, what types of evidence there are, and how to find logical explanations for strange occurrences. Please be advised that everything mentioned in this chapter are solely the beliefs of myself and are strictly theory. No one can truly become a professional in a field that has not yet to be even proven to exist 100 percent. There are charlatans out there who charge loads of money to gullible people for what are supposed to be "certifications" in paranormal investigating. Who in the hell are these people to give me a certificate made on a home computer and printed on gloss paper, telling me that I am now certified in a field that no one can prove. All I can give to you are my honest beliefs in regard to what I have personally experienced and what has been taught to me by those that have been studying the paranormal years before I have. After reading this, I'm afraid you won't be receiving any pretty little certificates nor any cute little ID badges said to allow you access in any cemetery at any given time of the night, without harassment from local law enforcement. Yes, there are actual people out there who do sell these items and people are dumb enough to fall for them. The famous P.T. Barnum couldn't have said it any better when he once said, "A sucker is born every day." Once the transaction is complete, the buyer soon finds out that his ID card is worthless, as he is being ran out of a private cemetery at 2:00 AM but by then, it's too late, as the con artist has already ran off with your hard earned money. Now that I got that off of my chest, on with a lesson in the paranormal.

I guess I will start with the one question that is asked to me the most: "What is a ghost?" From any sixth grade science class we are taught that everything living is made up of energy. As I type this, electrical impulses from my brain send signals to my eyes and hands. Those signals allow my fingers to move and my eyes to read what is being typed. My eyes then send those messages back to my brain and process them into an image. This is done all day long with any action we are performing. These impulses are with us from birth until the day we die. The million dollar questions remains: "Where does that energy go when we die?" Albert Einstein once said, "Energy never ceases to exist, it only changes form." Taking that into consideration, what does this released energy turn into once it is released? Theory is that when we die, that stored energy is released into the atmosphere. Depending on how the individual died, the energy is released in specific intervals. The best analogy I can give for this is if you were to take a balloon and slowly let the air out. If someone dies a slow and natural death, their energy is slowly released into the atmosphere. Taking that same balloon and sticking it with a needle can be compared to an individual who has died a sudden and traumatic death. As with the air in the balloon, that energy is suddenly released, causing an imprint in time, so to speak.

Other factors, such as the amount of electromagnetic energy in the surrounding area, are said to literally serve as a force field, containing that energy in a particular area. It is often rumored that locations set in an area located near large amounts of quartz can also serve as a recording device of sorts. Quartz has, what is called, piezoelectric properties, which means that the crystals can develop electrical potentials when placed under a mechanical stress. Quartz is also said to have recording capabilities. Qualities such as these often cause paranormal enthusiast to believe that large amounts of quartz, say in a mountainous area, can literally store this energy, serving as a tape recorder set on repeat. An example of this is the famous Mitchell-Hedges Skull that was found in 1926 under a collapsed temple in Belize. The near flawless skull is said to be created using no tools and was carved with mere sand over a period of 100 to 300 years. The skull is said to possess supernatural and healing powers, yet there is no verified validity to these claims.

Specific dates are also said to be catalysts for hauntings. Many locations go all year without anything strange taking place until a specific date rolls around, such as a birthday, wedding anniversary, or death. My cousin, whose father died when he was eight, would often tell me that every year around the time of his death, he would experience something strange. He told me stories ranging from occurrences such as a coffee pot brewing coffee on its own, all the way to seeing the shadowed figure of his father walking down the hallway. However, these events only would take place around the anniversary of his death.

People often ask me, "Why are spirits trapped here on earth?" I am not so sure that I would say that any spirit is necessarily trapped here. In most cases, a true intelligent haunting, which I will explain in greater detail later, stays in one particular area because it is either staying behind to relay some sort of message to the living, linger around for what they feel is unfinished business, or has some sort of attachment to a place and/or person. In some cases, the spirit doesn't even know they are deceased, simply going about their own business as when they were living.

To get a better understanding of a haunting, one must differentiate between the different types. The types range from mere etches in time to the really nasty stuff that no one wants to ever encounter. In theory, the types of hauntings are: residual, intelligent, poltergeist, demonic, and living apparitions. Once again, I must slap up the disclaimer that these are my opinions and may, or may not, be the same as yours so bear with me.

A residual haunting is said to be the most commonly occurring type of haunting. I would not call a residual a true haunting, for the anomaly is simply an etching in time, literally like a tape player. There is no true spirit present during the event, only the residual energy left behind, normally caused by a traumatic event or a replay of an event performed by the individual when he/she was living, literally on a daily basis. The entity has no knowledge that you are there, nor does it have a personality. It simply replays a specific event over and over again. An example of this, I once spoke with an individual who claimed to see an elderly man walking down her hallway. The man made no acknowledgments to the homeowner, as he simply would walk down the hall and fade into the wall. The interesting thing was that the house was built off the ground and when the man was seen walking, it appeared as if he was walking on the ground because his waist area ran flush with the floor. When researching history on the home, the woman found that there was a house located on the property years ago that belonged to an elderly man. In addition, the house was built on the ground, explaining for the strange "decapitated" effect. The man continued being seen walking the same path at recurring intervals, never making any acknowledgments to the homeowner.

This is often the type of haunting that is easiest to deal with, as I simply tell the homeowners there is absolutely nothing to worry about, as I explain to them that the event is simply an etching in time. I have never dealt with people that, after being educated, didn't become accustomed to the residual activity, literally making it a part of their daily lifestyle. In many cases, the energy simply dissipates over time.

Intelligent hauntings are my personal favorite. These are the spirits who know where they are, know that you are there, and do not mind making their presence known. They can be benevolent or mischievous, and rarely harmful. Still, as with the living, there are good people and there are pure jerks. When these people die, not much will change their personality. A person who was an easy-going practical joker will most likely yield a mischievous spirit. The same goes for the person who was always grumpy when they were living. They will make for a feisty, unfriendly spirit. Whatever the case may be, both will initially frighten an unknowing homeowner. In many cases, as with the residual, the homeowners are just afraid of the unknown and even though the entity is not there to cause any harm, its mere presence is enough to send the individuals in a panic. Other times, even if the spirit is legitimately causing a scare, it may be because the homeowner is doing something to unintentionally antagonize it. The most common things done that cause this uprising are excessive noise and remodeling. When these actions cease, so does the spirit. One of the first questions I ask a potential client is if they have been doing any recent remodeling of their homes. In many of the cases they are doing some sort of remodeling and that is when they noticed a spike in strange occurrences. I can only theorize that the reason behind this is by having the homeowner change the appearance to an area that was once so familiar to the spirit, they are simply ticked off that someone is messing with their property. As I mentioned, in many cases, the spirits are unaware they are dead and may be wondering, "Who are these people in my house?"

Intelligent hauntings are said to be most active between the hours of 11:00 PM and 4:00 AM. The reason for this is that these are the darkest hours of the night. The darker it is, the less energy the spirit requires to manifest. For example, take a flashlight and turn it on in the middle of the day. You will barely be able to see the light. However, if you take that same flashlight and turn it on at two in the morning, that light will be much more visible. Many people ask us why we conduct our investigations at night. Besides the reason I just mentioned, another good reason is that in the dark, with the loss of our eyesight, all of our other senses become greatly enhanced, enabling us to hear noises that we normally wouldn't have heard during the day. In addition, it has been proven that sound waves travel easier and farther in the dark.

In regards to abilities, an intelligent haunting is not very strong, as it can only move objects ten pounds or less. Due to the fact that they are not inhuman, religious provocation usually does not work, despite what the homeowner thinks. Whether they are attached to a certain artifact, trying to get a message to someone, or simply do not want to leave, once the reason for their presence is discovered, one can often alleviate the problem by either getting rid of the object or simply telling the spirit, "You are not welcomed here." It sounds simple, but you would be surprised at how many cases I have seen taken care of by simply having the homeowner stand their ground and telling the spirit to leave. I have often heard stories from years back when people did not trust putting their money in banks so they would bury their savings in a hidden place, normally next to a tree. When the individual would die, their spirit would come back to give the message to a loved one on where they could find the money. Once the money was found, the haunting would cease.

Poltergeist, the German word for "noisy spirit", is one of the more debated types of hauntings. No one is for certain what causes a poltergeist, or what gets rid of one. Some feel that poltergeists are simply a stronger version of an intelligent haunting. Others feel that a poltergeist is psychosomatic in nature, unconsciously caused by an individual's own emotional tensions. Theory is that a poltergeist also tends to focus around pre-teen girls and mentally handicapped adults. The reason for this is that their sexual energy is either unused or untapped. I have to throw in a joke on this one because if unused sexual energy is the cause for a chair moving, then most married men could have their lawn mowed without getting off the couch. Whatever the cause, poltergeist can effect an entire household, yet normally focus around one individual. The activity begins and ends very quickly and can range from days to years. The types of things that occur with a poltergeist escalate with time and have been classified into the following five levels:

Level 1: Known as the "senses attack" because in this early stage, the poltergeist will simply cause unknown sounds, strange smells, cold spots, and strange animal activity.

Level 2: Basically the same as level 1, except all the above mentioned occurrences are slightly enhanced, such as laughing or moans, visible shadows, strange mists, and areas of enhanced static electricity.

Level 3: This is where the poltergeist truly makes its presence known by physically interacting with objects near you such as opening/closing doors, turning on/off lights, and unseen hands touching or grabbing people.

Level 4: Now the poltergeist is beginning to get dangerous. It now begins to feed off of emotions and fears, using them to increase the terror level in the home. Objects will begin to get thrown across the room, feelings of dizziness or nausea will take place, items will levitate, fires will mysteriously start, and entities will begin to appear.

Level 5: This is when a poltergeist is at its strongest and most dangerous. It will begin to show violence and threatening behavior such as slapping or hitting, using inanimate objects to cause harm, blood on walls will appear, and in the most severe cases, possession can take place. As mentioned, these activities can last from days to years. Once level 5 has been achieved, at any given time, the activity can stop completely, starting all over at level 1 and increase accordingly.

I once read of a case involving a private residence somewhere in the Mid East portion of the country. In this case, the homeowner experienced nearly all the signs of a poltergeist that I mentioned above and she was now beginning to fear for the life of her and her daughter. She had a group of paranormal investigators come to her house, along with a camera crew, to document the event. While there, they witnessed a flower that was on her window sill completely singed around the edges, as if it were lit on fire. They then filmed a strange pinkish substance that began to ooze from the walls. The substance was collected and taken to a lab, where it tested positive for human plasma.

One of the more publicized accounts of a possible poltergeist was the infamous Bell Witch Haunting in Adams, Tennessee. The legend was that a man, John Bell, was cursed by a local "witch", causing him and his family to be constantly tormented, especially his youngest daughter, Betsy. Many who have studied the case strongly feel that the haunting was not a witch's curse, but actually a poltergeist generated from Betsy's very own psyche and her personal mental problems. Whatever the case may be, all the accounts stated that the entire household was harmed by this entity, but a majority of the activity centered on Betsy.

Demonic hauntings are reported to be the most dangerous, yet fortunately rare, types of haunting there are. Going back long before biblical times, there have been reports of good versus evil. A demonic haunt is extremely serious, as its only motives are causing ill-will towards mankind. Characteristics of a demonic haunt are sulfuric odors, growls, and pockets of warm air. They are most often seen as black shadow figures and half-man, half-animal creatures. They can change shape and appearance instantly; to conform to the individual(s) they are attempting to wreak havoc on. They are extremely strong and do not mind expressing their strength by hitting or scratching people. Religious provocation and/or an extremely skilled and legitimate sensitive seem to be the only ways to clear a demonic haunting. However, it may take several attempts, as after the first few tries, it could only tick it off even more and/or it will purposely lay low for a while, giving you the impression that it has been taken care of, only to return when you least expect it.

Another trait of a demonic haunting that makes it so dangerous is that it enjoys targeting young children. They will often make themselves known to the child at a very early age in the form of another child or someone that can easily befriend them. A sign of this is that the young child will begin talking about an imaginary friend. Of course this, in itself, is nothing unusual, as most children have imaginary friends that they play with. It doesn't become questionable behavior until the child begins to tell outlandishly detailed stories about the "friend", giving information such as strange names and history that a normal child of that age could not simply make up. The demon's motive is simply to gain as much trust as they can in this child, slowly eating away at its freewill until, most commonly, the pubescent years arrive. At this time, the haunting either completely dissipates or turns into full-blown possession.

People are often curious as to why children seem to be more susceptible to seeing spirits, regardless of their threat level. Theorists believe that this is due to the Pineal Gland, also known as "The Third Eye." Located deep in the center of the brain, the Pineal Gland is said to initiate supernatural powers allowing those to reach a higher plane. The gland is said to be larger in children, hence the increased susceptibility, then begins to shrink until the child reaches puberty. It is said that continued meditation and relaxation techniques can exercise the gland, allowing it to function in the adult years. It is also said that a head trauma can reactivate the use of the Pineal Gland. Currently, I am working on a case where the individual has recently had brain surgery. Prior to the surgery, they would occasionally see strange things that they could not explain. However, after the surgery, they have noticed a tremendous increase in strange phenomena seen. I am looking into the possibilities of whether or not the surgery could have affected the gland.

Living apparitions, also known as Dopplegangers, are the rarest form of haunting. Dopplegangers, which is German for "double walker", are said to be an exact replica of a living individual. It is said that only the owner of the doppelganger can see this phantom self, and that it can be a harbinger of death. Occasionally, however, a doppelganger can be seen by a person's friends or family, resulting in quite a bit of confusion. In instances of bilocation, a person can either spontaneously or willingly project his or her double, known as a wraith, to a remote location. This double is indistinguishable from the real person and can interact with others just as the real person would. A well known account of this if from the mid-1800's, as a thirteen year old Latvian student, witnessed the living apparition of her teacher, as it stood next to him, mimicking his every move while he wrote on the blackboard. This sighting was also verified by the thirteen other students that were present that day. Still, as with any strange occurrence, science must always play a part. In 2006, Swiss college students ran various tests on an individual and felt that they were able to recreate the effects similar to that of a living apparition. The students felt that if the left temporal region of the brain was disturbed, then the patient could get the sensation of a foreign presence, much like mental disorders such as schizophrenia and paranoia.

Now that I have touched on the basis of a haunting as well as the different types, we must now move on to explaining the different forms of actual evidence that can validate paranormal activity. There are many types of evidence that can be collected showing that there are signs that something strange is going on. Despite stereotypical mental pictures of floating bed sheets, paranormal evidence can range from a slight mist to an actual solid human figure. Some of the types I will discuss are: apparitions, orbs, electromagnetic fields, electronic voice phenomena, ectoplasm, and instrumental trans-communication.

What better piece of evidence to start with than orbs, which is the most controversial type of evidence. I really feel that the word "orbs" should officially become a new dirty four-letter word. I am so sick of hearing about orbs I think I will have diarrhea on myself next time the topic comes up. Everywhere I go, every class I teach, and every investigation I go on, I am shown numerous pictures of what people feel are orbs. In 99 percent of the photos I am shown, the orbs are simply reflections of dust or moisture particles, especially if the pictures are taken outside. Of the mere 1 percent that are actually legitimate orbs; people still do not realize that an orb is simply a collection of energy. Just because you have captured a quality orb, does not mean you have evidence of a ghost. Sure, orbs are usually present when an entity is around but it's not always the case vice versa. One theory

I have heard, and respect, is in regards to the phenomena of Electromagnetic Luminaries (ELMs), stating that they are balls of electrostatic energy literally having a mind of their own. This is said to be the first step in the formation of an apparition. When I teach paranormal classes, I am often asked to discuss the difference of a real orb and dust. I have heard many try to give a long drawn out description of a real orb as having such characteristics as a nucleus center, misshapen form, and/or blue in color. I highly disagree with such descriptions, as people are just trying too hard to pull blood from a turnip. They are simply so desperate to get evidence of the paranormal in an attempt to get "one up" on the next group, that they find themselves discrediting the reputation of their group. A legitimate orb is one that literally emits its own light source, highly resembling the definition of the above mentioned ELMs.

When taking photographs on an investigation, it is highly recommended that you strictly critique them before sending them out for second-party opinions. Someone may have photographed what they feel is a legitimate orb, yet after I explain to them that if it is very faint and only a vague circle is visible, it is dust. Some also report seeing a face or a skull in the "orb", as that is simply a logically-explained phenomenon called "matrixing", which we will explain later. Finally, please do not take a picture in a room that you know is full of dust and still claim to have ten to fifteen orbs in the shot. I was once sent a photograph taken right in front of central air vent. The vent blew dust all in the shot, looking like it was snowing, yet the sender still had their mind set that they captured an orb fest. I'm sure I am coming off as a completely skeptical jerk, especially in the eyes of the hardcore believers that would take the smell of flatulence and say it's a sign of a demonic haunting. However, I firmly feel that to be considered credible, than you must be your own hardest critic. Trust me, as you will see later in the book, if you aren't, there are a million and one people out there who will slam your evidence to the ground.

Ectoplasm is another highly debatable form of evidence. True ectoplasm is said to be the substance secreted from the manifestation or dissipation of a spirit. However, this is one of the easiest forms of evidence to fabricate, as cigarette smoke and breath on a cold night can give off the same appearance as vaporous ectoplasm. Anytime I am sent a photograph of supposed ectoplasm, I have to always throw it out for the simple fact that I was not there to take the picture myself. Even if the photo was not intentionally staged, people can still accidentally capture breath or cigarette smoke that was not visible with the naked eyes. It is extremely important that when you are on an investigation, you do not smoke.

If the weather is cold outside, be sure to hold your breath for a few seconds prior to taking the picture. If you have taken the above mentioned precautions and still have captured an unknown vaporous mist, begin taking as many pictures as you can in all directions, while checking for sudden temperature fluctuations in the nearby area.

The next type of evidence I will discuss is an electromagnetic field (EMF). EMFs are invisible lines of force found in all electrical devices. Even when most of these devices are turned off, as long as they are still connected to a power source, they will emit a readable level of EMFs, normally transferred to gauss and millagauss. From a ghost hunter's perspective, EMF's can potentially represent the manifestation of a spirit. In theory, researchers feel that the conscious mind emits its own electromagnetic field. It is believed that the field remaining from the brain waves is the only thing that can survive bodily death. EMF meters are used to detect these sudden fluctuations in magnetic fields.

To get an increase in electromagnetic energy alone does not mean that you have definite proof of paranormal activity. As stated, many household appliances emit their own EMFs and will often give off false readings. Other regular causes for false readings are poorly-insulated electrical wiring, cell phones, and two-way radio transmissions. All this must be taken in account when conducting EMF base readings on an investigation, which we will discuss in more detail later.

Another important thing to remember when dealing with EMFs are the dangers derived from overexposure to unhealthy levels of the fields. Tests have shown that regular exposure to high levels of EMFs can cause symptoms such as nausea, dizziness, paranoia, and, in extreme cases, even hallucinations. I have worked several cases where the clients have reported feeling uneasy in certain areas of their home. Upon investigating, it was determined that there were extremely high levels of EMFs found in the same areas where the uneasy feelings were felt. Normally, this took place in older homes where there were exposed breaker boxes and electrical wiring that was old and not insulated well. It is simple scientific research like that that can calm down a scared homeowner, not knowing what is going on in their home. What they once thought was a harmful spirit has now been clarified as high levels of EMF energy. Like I said earlier, to be an effective investigator, you must research several different fields, some of which have nothing to do with the paranormal. Yet, in the long run, it will make you and your group extremely reputable and respected.

The next type of evidence is the full-blown apparition, said to be the "holy grail" for all paranormal investigators. This ever so elusive type of evidence is simply the video or photographic evidence of a solid or translucent human figure. As mentioned earlier, an apparition is said to begin its formation by the presence of an electromagnetic luminary. These balls of light then gather to form an ectoplasmic mist, then ultimately forming into a human form. As I said, the apparitions can range from being very vague, translucent images of an individual, all the way to a completely solid figure that looks like you or I.

My favorite type of paranormal evidence would have to be electronic voice phenomena, or EVPs. EVPs are said to be the disembodied voices from spirits beyond the grave. They have diligently been studied since the early 1800's by such notorieties as Thomas Edison. After obtaining several strange recordings during his many audio experiments, Edison believed that a device could in fact be designed to record voices from the grave, yet there is no documented proof that he ever did create such a device. It wasn't until the mid 1900's when American photographer, Attila Von Szalay began experimenting with reel-to-reel tape recorders, successfully capturing what he felt were voices of deceased individuals. From there, the interest in EVPs skyrocketed, as people began to design devices that they though could record spirits while others established groups, solely devoted to the study and research of the phenomena.

No one is quite certain as to how EVPs are created. Paranormal believers feel that they are created by spirits who are actually causing an imprint on the audio recording devices by means that are not yet discovered. Skeptics feel that the sounds being heard are simply easily explainable occurrences such as CB radio interference and even a cross-contamination of AM/FM radio signals. Speaking from experience, while doing some audio recordings at a private residence near a radio station, I actually captured several seconds of the radio feed on my recorder. I was able to hear the DJ's voice as well as a brief section of music so I know for a fact that this interference can take place. Another logical explanation given by skeptics is called auditory pareidolia, which is when the recording is simply the result of one's mind playing tricks on them, finding indecipherable sounds and subconsciously turning them into words. This event causes the human brain to incorrectly interpret random patterns as being random sounds of the human voice. However, over the years, there have been legitimate studies conducted by valid scientists in regards to EVPs. Some of these tests were in regard to the frequency that the actual recording was taken from. The human voice is capable of transmitting frequencies anywhere between 300 mhz and 1000 mhz. In many cases, there have been voices recorded well below or above that range, suggesting that the sounds were not made by the human voice. Could spirits be communicating on a different frequency, such as that of a dog whistle, where our ears cannot pick them up?

Another type of evidence, very familiar to EVPs, yet not as widely known, is called instrumental trans-communication, or ITC. ITC is said to be a plain of communication for spirits by means of electronic devices such as televisions, computers, and fax machines. Unlike EVPs, ITC does not rely solely on audio and primarily involve visual images being transmitted on the above mentioned electronic devices. From evidence I have personally seen, ITC generates some of the more amazing images around, being extremely clear and detailed. In one case, a close friend of mine was taking a picture of his cat, which was sleeping on top of his big screen TV, which was turned off at the time. When the picture was viewed, the TV looked as if it was turned on, generating a very clear image of a young man standing in what appeared to be a small apartment. Those who viewed the picture immediately assumed that the television was turned on at the time, due to the fact that the image was so clear. The amazing thing was that once my friend's wife viewed the picture, she was in shock, as the man in the image was, in fact, her cousin who had passed away several weeks prior to the picture being taken.

In case you are wondering how to experiment with ITC, it is quite simple. Simply take a video camera and connect it to a TV using the supplied video plug, allowing you to simultaneously see everything that is being filmed on the television. Next, turn the video camera towards the television, giving an infinite loop of a picture, in a picture, etc. It is theorized that this strange frequency caused from this infinite loop is similar to the frequency that spirits can communicate on. Record several minutes of this strange, psychedelic-looking image and then play it back one frame at a time. I must warn you in advance, the one time I tried this, it gave me one hell of a headache, watching the constant flipping of the screen. However, some of the results I have seen from others who have tried it are simply incredible. I have heard that there are some negatives to doing this, as the possible risk of opening a portal exists. A portal is said to a gateway for spirits to travel in and out of, allowing both complacent and negative spirits direct access into the area. Old school investigators will also tell you that other catalysts for possible portal formations are having mirrors face one another in a room and/or having a lit candle in front of a mirror. I love working with the older investigators that have been doing this all of their lives, as I have learned so many different wives-tales, so to speak, that has been handed down from generation to generation, much of which cannot be found in any paranormal how-to book.

5

TOOLS OF THE TRADE

When discussing tools of the trade, I could literally go on forever, as there is such a wide array of tools used by paranormal investigators. The list could range from simple intuition all the way to electronics costing thousands of dollars. Whatever the case may be, the arsenal used by each investigator is unique to their likings. When speaking with older investigators, the only tools they mentioned was an old Polaroid camera, a candle, and a sink full of water. According to them, they would place a lit candle in a room where there were no air currents present. They would carefully monitor the flame for sudden changes. If the flame would begin to substantially dance around and/or grow in size, it was a sign that a spirit was present. They would also look to see if the flame would change color, as specific colors could also tell the investigator the disposition of the entity. Another trick I have heard being used in the past was filling a sink full of water and then allowing it to drain. Normally, water drains in a clockwise direction. However, if water was observed draining in a counter-clockwise direction, that was also a sign of a strange presence. I really am not sure how much accuracy there was in these methods and techniques, which is why I rely heavily on various types of electronic and recording devices, in an attempt to obtain legitimate proof of paranormal activity. It's still too early in the book for me to knock groups who rely solely on sensitive individuals for their investigative findings, but I find you can become much more reputable if you have just one simple recorded piece of evidence, as opposed to one or two people saying they felt something strange in a particular area during the night. To give you a brief introduction of the various pieces of equipment I use when investigating, I will discuss the uses for thermal imaging cameras, CCTV surveillance systems, EMF meters, digital cameras, voice recorders, thermometers, and video cameras.

Thermal imaging cameras are on every investigator's "wish list" because of their amazing capabilities. Thermal imaging is useful in many occupations such as firefighting and plumbing and is also a very important tool used by the military. All objects emit some sort of infrared radiation, reflecting different levels of heat. A thermal imaging camera is capable of detecting this wide range of temperatures radiating from these objects in real time video. The reason this tool has been so sought after by paranormal investigators is that it is used to detect the slightest bit of temperature changes caused by the manifestation of a spirit. Even if they are not visible, their mere presence is said to still radiate some sort of heat. Thermal cameras have been used to capture such anomalies as full-bodied apparitions, strange mists, and even footsteps left behind by an unknown presence.

There are some negative concerns when using thermal cameras. One of the biggest downsides is the cost of the unit, which can range from $5,000 to $50,000. However, if you are interested in purchasing one, I highly recommend not buying the lowest-end model you can find simply to say you have a thermal camera. Most importantly, I would suggest getting one that has a video output, as opposed to one that is only capable of taking still photographs. By getting one with a video output, you can connect it to any handheld video camera and record the video feed in real time. In addition to the high price tag, yearly cleaning and calibration is needed, which also is expensive. Another issue is the time it takes to properly train in the field of thermography. Due to the camera's extreme sensitivity, you will receive many false positives such as heat trails from large insects, your own reflection in a mirror, and the heat left behind on a chair. To the untrained eye, many of these images will have you believing that you have captured something paranormal when, in all actuality, it is something easily explainable. Despite the downsides, using one is simply amazing. The times I have been fortunate enough to work with one, I was thoroughly impressed with its capabilities.

One of the more useful pieces of electronics used is the infrared camera. Our eyes are capable of seeing everything in the color spectrum such as red, orange, yellow, green, blue, and violet. This leaves the other levels of light in the electromagnetic spectrum that are invisible to the naked eyes such as gamma rays, x-rays, ultraviolet, radio waves, microwaves, and infrared. Theoretically, you are more susceptible to observing a spirit or an orb through infrared levels of light. An IR camera is basically a standard color video camera with anywhere from 12–200 small LED (light-emitted diodes) surrounding the lens. When the level of light reaches a specific darkness, a small sensor activates the diodes. From this point on, everything seen is through infrared light. One of the biggest downsides to this is the fact that every single piece of dust will be quite visible, looking like a damn orb fest on screen. Bugs will also interfere a great deal with IR cameras as they will also give the impression of a strange anomaly. The key is for you to educate yourself on the characteristics of dust, bugs, and legitimate orbs. Dust, regardless of how bright it is, will float in the picture and then slowly float out. Sometimes, with strange air drafts, the dust will make sharp turns or curve into a particular room which, to an untrained eye, is often mistaken for an orb. Bugs are a little easier to detect as their movements are very sporadic and, if the bug is large enough, you can often see the fluttering of the wings. Legitimate orbs on camera will appear to have a mind of their own, making several sudden changes in flight, interact with those present, and/or emit a visible light source.

Luckily, IR cameras are fairly affordable, as you can get a quality one for about $70–$100. When shopping, the two main features to look at are the lines of resolution and the lens size. The lines of resolution are basically the quality of the image taken by the camera. Personally, I would not get a camera with no less than 420 lines and no more than 520. The lens size tells you how much area coverage the camera will capture. The lower the number, the more area you can cover. I made the mistake once of purchasing a camera with great image quality and tons of led's yet found out that it had an 8mm lens on it, which basically zoomed everything in so much, I could only use the camera for extremely long hallways. I highly recommend getting a camera with no more than a 3.5mm or 4mm lens on it. A secondary feature that is important is the amount of led's on the camera. Obviously, the more lights on the camera, the brighter and further it will see in complete darkness. When setting up the camera for surveillance, be sure to securely mount it on a tripod and face it in an area that will allow you to cover the largest possible area. Be sure that you do not put two cameras facing one another because the IR lights, although showing a faint red glow to the naked eye, will appear as a large spotlight when viewing it through the infrared level.

Now that you have a nice IR camera up and running, you will need some sort of recording device to save the video. Please don't try and use your mom's 1988 VCR to record your camera footage, as you will lose valuable quality and it is simply tacky. I cannot emphasize enough how beneficial it is to get a digital video recorder. A DVR is simply a recording device that enables you to link several cameras together on one screen, while simultaneously recording all of the video to a built-in hard drive. DVRs range anywhere from $150–$2,000, depending on the amount of channels it has and the size of its hard drive. CCTV surveillance DVRs come in 4, 8, 16, 32, and 64 channel capacities. For single-channel DVR home systems, in order to view 4 screens at the same time, you will have to purchase what is called a quad processor. Costing about $80, a quad processor will enable you to link the four cameras into the single-channel DVR via the video input and then onto your monitor for viewing.

Another useful tool used by investigators is an EMF meter. As mentioned earlier, electromagnetic fields are invisible lines of energy said to accompany the manifestation of a spirit. An EMF meter is used to detect these fluctuations in energy, possibly finding its source. In most cases, the meter is useful in simply finding natural sources such as faulty wiring and breaker boxes. This is normally done when conducting the initial base readings on either a preliminary or at the beginning of an actual investigation. During this time, all areas of the investigation location are scanned in order to obtain our base readings. In an area that has literally no electrical devices, a base reading of approximately 0.0–0.2 gauss would be established. During the investigation, if a reading substantially higher than that is obtained, and there is no explanation as to what caused this spike, then there could be the possibility that there is a paranormal presence. This is why it is absolutely essential that base readings are obtained prior to the actual investigation. By doing this, you will know exactly where the explainable pockets of high EMFs are, keeping you from getting false readings when you are caught in the moment during an investigation.

When shopping around for a meter, there are many makes and models to choose from. The most important thing to remember, as with any electronic, is "you get what you pay for." Don't always settle for the cheapest meter out there, as you will basically end up with a piece of crap. The cheapest meter I would suggest is about $45 and it is called the K-II meter. It is very simple to operate, having five diodes of different colors. The stronger the EMF present, the more lights that will light up. The one thing that is aggravating is that you have to constantly keep your thumb on the button the entire time. After a while, your thumb gets tired and you will start to ease off the button which actually will cause a brief spike on the meter, giving a false reading. To alleviate this problem, I simply insert a dime into the slot, keeping the button depressed the entire time. Recently, I have been hearing a lot of negative comments on the use of a K-II meter for the simple fact that you can manipulate the readings so easily. Still, for the beginning investigator wanting to have fun learning and not go broke in the process, I still would recommend the K-II.

For the novice investigators wanting to spend a little more for a more accurate meter, then I would recommend a single-axis digital meter. Costing approximately $80, this meter is far more accurate than the K-II due to the fact that it has a digital screen, giving you the exact level of the EMFs present. One downside of the device is that it is a single-axis, which means that the meter is reading from only one point of origin. If you barely shake the meter or move it abruptly, such as walking up stairs, you will get a false reading. Another downside is that the LCD screen on the meter is not backlit, requiring you to constantly keep a flashlight on the screen to monitor the readings. However, I have often seen people attach a small map light to the back of the meter to illuminate the screen. One thing I use that emits a less harsh light than the map light is a miniature chemical light stick. They are approximately two inches in length and are used in night fishing. I simply snap two of them, activating the chemical, and tape one on the top of the screen and the other on the bottom, giving just enough light to read the meter during an investigation. Leave it up to a Coonass to always engineer something like that. I can remember when I was young, my dad would take an egg beater and tie it to the end of a broomstick, making a device that would effectively pick up pecans off the ground. Although it looked ridiculous, the damn thing worked. Got to love those Cajuns.

My favorite of EMF meters would have to be the tri-field meter. Costing $120 for a base model and $190 for one with a built-in alarm, a tri-field meter is extremely accurate and sensitive. The device operates on a triple-axis basis, meaning that it obtains its samples from various angles for a much more detailed reading. It is well worth it to opt for the one with the built-in alarm, as you do not have to constantly keep your eyes on it. Simply set the alarm to sound at a certain reading and listen for it to go off. If you have decided that you will get a tri-field meter, I must warn you in advance not to accidentally get the natural EMF meter. They look identical and cost the same, yet the natural meter is much too sensitive for paranormal investigative purposes. For instance, the tri-field meter can give readings up to 200–300 gauss, while the natural meter maxes out at only 3 gauss, which basically means you will stay maxed out the entire time during an investigation. Studies have shown that a natural EMF meter is so sensitive; it can detect a bolt of lightning up to seven miles away and will actually give slight fluctuations based on your own EMF energy.

Now that you have purchased whichever meter you have chosen, it is time to learn how to use it. Regardless of which meter you have chosen, they are all fairly easy to operate. The most important things to remember with any meter are that you keep your hand as steady as possible, moving it in a sweeping motion side to side and up and down, and don't freak out if it jumps a few tenths of a gauss. Remember, due to wiring and electrical devices, each room can have a different base reading. One room can have a base of 0.2 gauss and another room may jump to 0.7 gauss simply due to its proximity to anything ranging from a breaker panel to a wireless router. As I mentioned, once your base reading has been obtained, the key is to look for sudden changes in excess of 1–2 gauss. Finally, I cannot reiterate how important it is to make sure that all cell phones are turned off during an investigation. Simply putting the phone on vibrate will not suffice, as the phone is constantly updating itself with local towers, causing an EMF spike.

Another handy tool is an infrared thermometer, which is used to detect surface and air temperatures. As mentioned earlier, for an entity to manifest, it requires energy. In many instances, it will pull energy from batteries, such as the instance during my first Ft. Derussy visit. Other times, the entity can draw the required energy from ourselves, leaving us feeling drained after an encounter. However, in a majority of the situations, energy is derived from the surrounding air, causing a drastic temperature change. In most cases, the temperature will drop, unless you are dealing with a demonic haunting, whereas the temperature will raise a substantial amount. It is truly amazing to experience an unexplained cold spot.

For instance, you could be in a room that is 80 degrees and all of a sudden, find this one small pocket of cold air that literally feels like you put your hand in a deep freezer. Trust me, when you experience a true cold spot, you will definitely know it.

An infrared, or non-contact, thermometer operates by the use of a lens which focuses the energy onto a detector, which converts the energy to an electrical signal that can be displayed in units of temperature. It seems that an IR thermometer is used by almost every paranormal group around; however, I am not very fond of them for the simple fact that no matter what you are pointing at, you will get a reading based on the first object that the infrared beam touches. For example, if I am pointing the thermometer at a wall from five feet away, I will get a specific reading. If I point at the same wall standing from twenty feet, that reading will be considerably different due to the fact that there is more air between myself and the wall, affecting the temperature being read. This affects looking for cold spots drastically, as you never know the exact location of one. It is for these reasons that I highly recommend a thermocouple thermometer, which is simply a digital thermometer with a slender temperature probe affixed to it. The thermometer only gives a reading based on the ambient temperature of the air at the end of the probe, generating a much more accurate reading of a designated area. You will know exactly where a cold spot is and its exact temperature. When purchasing one, the key is to get one with a very slender probe, as the thicker ones will give you a more delayed reading.

One piece of equipment that tends to belong to every investigator is a simple digital voice recorder, which is used to capture the ever so popular electronic voice phenomena. Recorders come in various models, ranging in price from $20–$500. Trust me when I say that this is one device where it pays to spend a little extra money on. One of my favorite quotes is: "Your EVP is only as good as your recorder." EVPs are hard enough to capture as it is, much less having to battle with the hissing and crackling of a piece of crap recorder. When shopping around, I suggest looking into any recorder that has stereo capabilities. Your recordings will replay in amazing quality, making your EVPs that much more credible. Old school investigators will often opt for an analog tape recorder for whatever prehistoric reasons they have, although I have yet to find any positives using an analog over a digital recorder. With an analog, you have to worry about keeping an endless supply of fresh cassettes, as you must always use a new one to avoid a possible bleed-over in the recordings. Also, you must always use an external microphone to avoid the constant sound of the gears turning during your recording.

When using your voice recorder, there are several rules to follow. First, make sure that you have turned off any noisy electrical devices that may interfere with your recordings, such as air conditioners and dishwashers. Next, be sure that when you start recording, you introduce yourself along with the date, time, and location. This helps you keep track of who is in what location and at what time. It is also a very good idea for everyone who is present to announce every time they enter or depart that particular room. Doing this, will assist you in discarding sounds that you would have originally thought were unusual, if you wouldn't have known someone was in that room. Another helpful thing to do when beginning your recordings is to audibly commentate as you take a few steps or knock on several different surfaces in the surrounding area. This will help later on when you are reviewing the audio and you hear a strange noise. You can compare it to the sounds you made earlier to see if they compare, further assisting you in narrowing down your clips.

Once you begin to obtain your recordings, many investigators would tell you to ask standard questions such as "What is your name?", "Can you give us a sign of your presence?", and "Do you want us to leave?" In the past, I would have suggested doing the exact same thing, as even to this day, I often conduct my recordings this way. However, I have noticed over the last year or so, I have had more success obtaining quality EVPs by simply conversing with my fellow investigators and not rambling off the same boring questions over and over. I tend to wonder if this could be due to the possibility that the spirits feel more comfortable with you when the atmosphere is more relaxed and you are not drilling it with questions, or could it be that the spirit is simply acting like a five year old child, waiting to give a response when they are damn good and ready. Whatever the case may be, I highly recommend trying a little bit of both techniques. Begin your night by simply sitting back and conversing with your teammate regarding random topics. Tell a few jokes, have a few laughs, whatever it takes to set a comfortable mood. After a while of doing this, begin asking the above mentioned questions and see if you get a response.

One term that is often mentioned when working with voice recorders and EVPs is white noise. White noise is simply a random signal that has the same frequency throughout its entire bandwidth. As with white light, which encompasses all forms of visible light, white noise is comprised of all frequencies. White noise is often generated by using an FM radio that is set to a dead station. I have also seen investigators use something as simple as a constantly dripping faucet to obtain their "noise". As long as there is some sort of constant, repetitive sound of the same frequency, that sound can be considered white noise. The theory behind white noise is that the constant background noise assists the spirit in generating a sound. Personally, I am not a big fan of the use of white noise simply because it is one more thing that gets in the way of trying to review audio. Listening to a recording for four to six hours, consisting of a constant hiss, is enough to drive anyone insane.

Probably the most common item used by investigators is a digital camera, which is used with the hopes of photographing any of the forms of paranormal evidence that I mentioned earlier. There are really no substantial specifics to look for when shopping for a camera other than one with a fairly good zoom and at least 4 megapixels. Many people will debate on using a standard 35mm camera as opposed to digital. Both types have their pros and cons, yet for overall simplicity and abilities, a digital camera has the most functionality. While film is costlier, it is harder to fake, as you have the original negatives to compare it to. However, a digital camera has the capability to store many more pictures and you can instantly see your results after each picture is taken.

One of the rules to remember when taking photographs is if you have a camera strap or long hair, be sure to keep them out of the way of the lens area. All it takes is a single strand of hair or a dangling camera strap to cause the investigator to believe they have captured something paranormal. As mentioned earlier, be sure no one is smoking in your vicinity and briefly hold your breath if it is cold outside. This prevents any false ectoplasm-like pictures from being taken. If your camera has a nighttime mode, please try not to use it. I get so many pictures e-mailed to me of strange squiggly lights and smeared images, only to find out that they were due to an overexposed shutter set on night mode. When set on this mode, you must keep the camera very stable, as the slightest movement will give you a blurred effect. Another important thing to remember, as a courteous precaution, let those around you know when you are about to take a picture by simply saying, "Flash." There is nothing worse than having your eyes accustomed to being in the dark, only to have them shocked by a bright flash. Other than that, it's pretty much open game in regards to taking photographs during an investigation. Take as many as you can from any and all angles. I even tend to take many behind my back and around corners, in hopes of possibly catching a spirit off guard. Also, take numerous pictures of the same thing back to back. This way, if one of the pictures has something that looks strange, you can compare it to the other shots of the same thing to see if the possible anomaly was all in of the pictures.

Once you have taken your share of photos, now comes the painstaking process of going through all of them. Don't rush through the process, as it takes a very detailed eye to sometimes notice something that shouldn't be in the picture. Almost immediately, I am sure you will be introduced to the beloved orbs, as particles of dust will reflect light, giving off a spherical appearance. Insects are another thing that can make its way into a photograph and give the appearance of something paranormal. Hardcore believers have the gall to often call them "fairies." In one funny case, I was e-mailed a photograph from a woman who was guaranteeing that she had photographed the image of an actual angel. She was very adamant with her e-mail, stating that she had the photograph analyzed by "three legitimate sensitives" and all three verified that the photo was real. As soon as I opened the picture, I couldn't help but laugh hysterically, as her "angel" was simply a large mosquito. For those of you who have never spent a summer night in Louisiana, we are notorious for our massive mosquitoes, or should I say "angels."

Another concern when reviewing photographs is a phenomenon called matrixing. Matrixing is the mind's natural habit of looking for facial features in inanimate objects. For example, if you stare at the clouds for a while, you will begin to see faces and other objects. The same applies to photographs. If you look at a specific batch of branches or leaves long enough, your mind will often find what looks like faces in them. Tips to avoid matrixing issues are to disregard any faces that appear "cartoonish" in appearance and overlook faces that are created by overlapping objects, such as branches.

The last piece of equipment most commonly used is a standard video camera, which is very useful for simply documenting the night's investigation and to possibly capture that ever so elusive apparition. Handheld cameras come in various formats such as 8mm, Hi8, MiniDV, DVD, and HD, all of which are good for paranormal use. It is recommended to purchase one with some sort of night vision capability. However, the capability on any given camera is often not very strong for our use, which is why we often incorporate what is called an IR illuminator to the camera. The IR illuminator is a device with eight LED lights that simply assist the night vision capabilities further by amplifying the ambient light. They can be found for about $40 and are well worth the money.

Now that you have been given a thorough lesson on how to investigate, what to look for, and how to use the equipment, all that is left is for you go out and "hunt dem ghosts." Despite all that I mentioned, remember that the most important thing is to go out and have fun. If you are out to just have a good time with friends with the hopes of possibly getting legitimate evidence, you don't have to go out and spend thousands of dollars on equipment. A simple flashlight, camera, and voice recorder are all that the recreational hunter needs. Start out simple by visiting a public cemetery at night. Make sure the cemetery is not posted and you are not trespassing after hours. It is also a good idea to simply notify the local police, telling them you will be there, for what reasons, and for how long. Sure, you may get a chuckle or two but in the end, it saves you a whole lot of hassle. Looking back, despite all of the historical places I have had the privilege of investigating, I cannot help but reminisce on those cemetery days when I was just starting out.

With all that said, I thank you for hanging in there with me as I introduced you to "Ghost Hunting 101". Whether or not you have read any paranormal how-to books before, I hope this section was informative enough to where you can take some of this information and apply it out there on the paranormal field. Regardless, I felt this section was a necessity in order to get everyone on the same page before I really get into the "meat and potatoes" of the book. From here on, there will be no more scientific explanations for some sort of fancy phenomena or electronic device. From this point on, everything will be told as it happened from the first day I decided I wanted to seriously become a paranormal investigator. About as proper as it will get is when I briefly break to give a detailed history and investigation report on each location I investigated. This is why I wanted to give this detailed "101" section first, so I wouldn't have to break momentum to explain what certain terms are. Now, when I mention the word "ectoplasm", you won't think it is the residue left behind from a "nocturnal emission".

6

THE MAKING OF A GHOST HUNTER

The days of bar-hopping with good old Jason had long passed, yet I would never forget that first visit to Ft. Derussy where I was nearly scared to death. Since a few years had passed, I had now become a father to a beautiful daughter named Olivia, became a career status employee with the Federal Bureau of Prisons, and returned to college to finish my degree in Computer Information Systems. Despite all the changes, I never lost my love for the paranormal. I continued reading as many books as I could, watched all the paranormal television programs that aired, and listened to all of the personal experiences of others. Still, I had yet to really begin to think about starting or joining an actual investigative group. I had absolutely no clue where to start nor how to find others to do this with me.

All these questions were answered on the day my wife would humorously call "the beginning of the end." At the time, I had a morning college class and was on my way back home during the local morning radio show. The discussion for that particular morning was, no other than, the paranormal. I quickly turned the radio up, as they discussed some of the local area hauntings such as the famous Bentley Hotel in Alexandria and Loyd's Hall Plantation in Cheneyville. The radio hosts proceeded to discuss a new nationally-televised program that would be starting that night. The show was going to be about a group of paranormal investigators that would investigate some of the most reportedly haunted locations in the country, using a more skeptic and scientific approach. One of the stars of this new program actually called into the show as he was questioned about what the show entailed. I was enthralled as this guy went into detail on how they would conduct their investigations, which was a method that interested me a great deal.

That night, I made it a priority to watch the program. What I watched was an extremely impressive program of everyday people like myself, who had an immense love for the paranormal. What really got my attention was their approach, which was that they would enter each investigation from a neutral standpoint, not immediately labeling each place as haunted. Their first and foremost goal was to actually attempt to debunk strange occurrences. Once any and all logical explanation had been exhausted, only at this time would they look into the paranormal. This was a breath of fresh air from many of the other shows I had watched, which basically consisted of a few "psychics" that would walk into a house, say they saw a little girl, and then supposedly communicate with it. None of this did me, or any of the other viewers, any good as I had to go off the "feelings" of these people. There was no concrete proof to validate what they were seeing or feeling. This new program was a breath of fresh air, as it appealed to skeptical believers such as myself. In addition, they used some pretty cool pieces of electronics, which quickly also appealed to me, as I am a technical nut.

The program was a quick success, as I never missed an episode, religiously watching it every week. I began to learn some of the techniques and lingo used by the investigators, incorporating it with what I had already learned from research and what was told to me by others. In the meantime, I had recently discovered several Louisiana-based Websites that were dedicated to listing some of the reportedly haunted locations in the state. Also, besides Jason, I had now found two other co-workers, Dustyn and Everett, which were equally interested in the paranormal. Needless to say, this was the fuel I needed to form my own small little paranormal investigative group.

First, I had to come up with a name. Being we were all from central Louisiana, I decided to go with "CenLa Paranormal Investigators". Looking back, I can't help but grin when I think of the motto I had come up with, which was "We put the sin back in CenLa." I'm sure that would have made for a real nice slogan on a business card when trying to investigate someone's home. Now that we had a name, I quickly ran to my computer to type out some sort of group layout. Being the anal person I am (Ok, that didn't sound too good.), I am a stickler for making lists and organizing things regardless of how small it may be. I then designed a pretty little letterhead which said, "CPI", and began to type up a list of duties for the group. I would have a case manager that would go out and look for places to investigate, a technical manager who would keep track of the equipment, and your regular investigators. Boy, did I think I was something or what.

Now came the hard part: Where can we investigate? Well it didn't take a rocket scientist to realize that we would stick with what worked for us and make our way back to Ft. Derussy. This would also give me a chance to redeem myself from my first visit there. I knew that if I wanted to become a legitimate investigator, I would have to get over that nervousness that had plagued me from that first visit. We then equipped ourselves with a basic flashlight and handheld video camera and headed to the cemetery. As we approached that infamous gravel road, I began to feel that ever-so-familiar nervousness that I had experienced the first time. Still, I was determined to face whatever it was that kept me from even stepping out of the vehicle last time. As we drove down the gravel road, Jason began to tell Dustyn the story of how scared I was on the initial trip, which began to lighten the mood a little.

As we made our way to the entrance of the cemetery, I was quickly hit with that "fight or flight" feeling, yet I continued to tell myself that there was no reason to be so intimidated. After all, it was just a cemetery. The three of us exited the vehicle and entered the cemetery. I constantly used the viewfinder of my video camera as my line of sight, as it seemed to desensitize me, giving me the feeling that I was watching everything on television. The night was extremely calm, with not a cloud in sight and a full moon that illuminated everything. It was one of those nights that you could maneuver around without a flashlight.

We walked around the cemetery for a while, reading the dates on all the headstones, trying to find the oldest ones. We made our way to the rear of the cemetery, which is the area that is roped off due to the unmarked graves. As we approached this spot, the three of us literally froze in our tracks, as we all felt this strange feeling encompass us. It wasn't a feeling of fear, but this subconscious suggestion, basically telling us that we shouldn't be there. I had overcome my nervousness, yet I was not going to tempt fate and overstay my welcome. We decided to leave my video camera running on its own while we went to obtain some "adult beverages" to calm our nerves. As we drove off, I had a huge feeling of self-gratification, knowing that I had just taken another step in becoming a paranormal investigator.

After about an hour, we returned to the cemetery to retrieve the video camera. I could not wait to start the review process, in the hopes that I may have caught the infamous "Devil's Run" on camera. I rushed home and began to go over the video, which proved to be a task in itself. For those of you who have never sat there and watched two to three hours of video, it can be quite tiring. To watch a video of a graveyard that has nothing moving, literally puts you in a hypnotized daze, as you slowly slip in and out of consciousness. After about forty-five minutes of watching the video, I began to doubt if I would catch anything or not. Suddenly, I saw this small ball of light literally bounce in from the left side of the screen. It paused a few times before it bounced off to the right, giving the impression that it had a mind of its own. I was absolutely elated to know that I may have actually captured something paranormal on my very first excursion. I quickly ran to Jason, Dustyn, and several other friends to show them this amazing piece of footage.

The video was quite dark due to the fact that I did not know about the importance of using an IR illuminator with a video camera. I decided to run the video through an editing program that would allow me to lighten the video up. What I found next shocked me. This extremely impressive light that I had captured was not the infamous Devil's Run or even an elusive *Feaux Follet*. The ball of light that raised my hopes up so much was the reflection off the eyes of a damn bull frog. I was so deflated, I felt like I child who had my dog ran over by a car. To make matters worse, my friends who I hyped the video up to, quickly made fun of my error. Already hesitant to accept my new found hobby, they had no problem with making sarcastic remarks, officially calling me "Ghost Buster". To this day, that name still follows me, especially with my co-workers and close friends.

Despite the disappointment from the discovery of the frog, there were mixed emotions, as part of me actually felt a sense of accomplishment. By taking the time to analyze the video and not quickly labeling it paranormal, I felt that I was taking an approach that not many groups were following. Unfortunately, this was one of the only outings by the short lived CPI. The group never took off as planned, leaving only myself and my immense interest in the hobby. Years later, a friend of mind form central Louisiana wanted to start his own group and asked me what I thought he should name it. As you can imagine, there was only one name that came to mind, as CenLa Paranormal Investigations was reborn. To this day, the group is still around, conducting small cemetery investigations, and it's good to see the name live on.

I knew that obviously I could not have a group that consisted of only one person so I began to look for other groups that I could possibly join. Unfortunately, my search came up empty handed so I returned to the comfort of reading as much on the topic as possible and watching my favorite paranormal investigating show, which had now become a huge hit and was already in its second season. As the season started, I was curious to see just what historical places they would be visiting. To my surprise, the episode I was watching was in Louisiana.

The episode consisted of the team meeting with another group called "Louisiana Ghost Hunters". The two teams would be joining forces to investigate a private residence said to be haunted by an extremely active spirit. According to the homeowner, every time he would bring home female company, the spirit became intensely jealous and would attack the female guests. The home was nearly two hundred years old and was built on a working sugarcane farm. The land was said to have also been the site of several Civil War skirmishes. The investigation portion of the program was conducted in the usual fashion, yielding some very impressive footage of a door opening and closing on its own.

Having new knowledge of this group in Louisiana, I knew this would be my chance to get my foot in the door. I quickly found the group's Website and began to look for contact information in regards to joining. I then typed up an extremely detailed e-mail, expressing my long time interest in the paranormal and how I was very interested in joining. I was certain that days later, I would be welcomed into the group and I would begin my exciting adventure as a legitimate paranormal investigator. One thing seemed to handicap those dreams; I never got a response. I am a firm believer in the saying "The squeaky wheel gets the grease", so I wrote another e-mail, expressing my interest in joining. Once again, I did not receive a response.

I then began to look for alternate routes to reach someone in this group. I noticed they had a message board so I quickly joined it and began to post introduction messages. The funny thing was, all the messages being posted were from people just like me. There were no actual group members present. It was as if these people had gone into seclusion after their few minutes of being nationally syndicated. I then began to wonder if the constant pestering was even worth it, especially if it was just going to fall on deaf ears. I decided to just lay low and continue to hang around on the message board, which was basically a purgatory for wanna-be ghost hunters who never had their e-mails acknowledged.

Just as I began to lose all hope, I received an e-mail from an individual named Steve Coleman. Steve was writing to tell me that he saw that I lived in Pineville, which was where he was originally from. He also said that he had recently joined the group and noticed I was interested in joining and would be willing to "put in a word for me." Steve proceeded to tell me that he knew of a few reportedly haunted locations in the Pineville area and would be more than willing to show them to me during his next visit up north. I was extremely excited knowing that I was getting closer to becoming part of an actual team. In anticipation for my meeting with Steve, I rushed out and purchased my first piece of equipment which was a K-II EMF meter. I would walk around like an idiot, conducting EMF sweeps in my house, just so I could watch it go off when I got close to my stove or microwave.

Steve and I continued to communicate back and forth with one another, discussing some of the different places we would like to investigate. A few weeks later, Steve called me and said that he was making his way up to Pineville and wanted to know if I wanted to go visit a local cemetery and Ft. Buhlow with him. Ft. Buhlow is a large earthwork fortification that was constructed by Confederate forces in October 1864. The fort received its name from its chief engineer, Lt. A. Buhlow and was constructed by 1,500 and 500 slaves. In anticipation of a third Red River Valley invasion by Federal troops, the fort was manned in March 1865, although no fighting ever took place.

Despite the fact that no major battles occurred, Ft. Buhlow has long been reported to be active. In addition to the grounds being site to a gigantic piece of Louisiana military history, it is also, ironically, a major spot for drug transactions and a popular make-out spot for the homosexual community. Needless to say, this was going to make for an interesting outing. After being advised of those useful bits of information, I grabbed my K-II and my .40 cal pistol and made my way to meet Steve for my first unofficial LGH investigation.

Meeting Steve, I immediately formed a liking to him, as he is extremely easy going and an overall great person. To this day, Steve remains extremely dedicated and I will always remember that I wouldn't be where I am at today if it wasn't for him. After we met, we headed towards an old Jewish cemetery in Pineville. We simply walked around and snapped a few pictures, experiencing nothing out of the ordinary. We then made our way down the street to Ft. Buhlow. Fortunately, crack transactions and "same-sex lovin" was not popular in the city of Pineville that night, as no one else was there when we arrived. We parked at the rest area and started walking around the fort, which is similar to Ft. Derussy, as it is simply a large earthen mound. I began to put my new K-II to use, conducting EMF sweeps all around the fort. As I approached a certain portion of the fort, I received two small spikes on the meter. There were no types of electrical devices around me to cause the increase, so I immediately became excited. Unfortunately, that was the only significant thing that happened while we were there.

Steve and I continued to speak over the phone, exchanging our stories as I continuously expressed my interest in becoming a member of LGH. Steve had spoke to the founders of the group on my behalf and they wanted me to meet with the case manager so he could get a feel for me as a person and an investigator. In the middle of this, the tragic event known as Hurricane Katrina struck the Louisiana coast, in between New Orleans and Biloxi. The devastation was unbelievable as it literally obliterated Biloxi and came very close to doing the same to New Orleans. Thousands were now homeless and began to try and find ways to rebuild their lives. Others decided to continue to live off of government aid and milk the system for what it was worth. They were shipped in busloads to middle and northern Louisiana where they were housed in temporary shelters. The crime rate began to soar almost instantly, as these hooligans began to pillage and trash the town. This left everyone running for the nearest gun shop, arming themselves in what looked like something out of a movie. Fortunately, this did not last long, as many of these fine citizens either moved elsewhere or returned to New Orleans.

Being that Steve was in the Army National Guard, he was sent to New Orleans to assist in the emergency aid that was being given in an area that was literally becoming a combat zone. What was an even more saddening thing was that while our own military and law enforcement were attempting to rescue stranded victims that were atop their roofs and airlifting infants off of the rooftop of the NIC unit at Charity Hospital, they were being shot at by our own civilians for absolutely no reason at all. This was taking place when, of course, they weren't looting the stores for fur coats in the summer and big screen televisions when New Orleans would not receive power until months later. I could continue on this forever but again, this would be a book in itself.

As I mentioned, with Steve gone for an undetermined amount of time, he put me in touch with the case manager for LGH. We spoke a few times over the phone and I continued to express my interest in joining. He then wanted to set up a meeting with me so we could speak face to face. We then set up a date and met one another, sharing our stories. He proceeded to tell me of a well known location in Sunset known as Marland's Bridge. According to him, this was a popular place for the paranormal enthusiasts to visit. Marland's Bridge is the site of the Civil War battle known as the "Battle of Bayou Bourbeau". The battle occurred on Tuesday, November 3, 1863. A large union camp of over 1,700 troops was camped on the western side of the bridge with union artillery on the north side. The battle itself started in the early morning hours around 4:00 AM, with the worst fighting around 1:00 PM. Union troops were taken completely by surprise by confederate troops that approached from the north, west, and southwest. In the midst of the panic, a large number of union troops tried to run while many others tried to form a defensive line to try and repel the attack. Total chaos erupted as the Texas Confederates descended on the Yankees. It was a total disaster for the union commanders.

Perhaps the only hero of the fiasco, and the man whom the bridge got its name, was twenty-three year old William Marland, a gunnery lieutenant in the 2nd Massachusetts artillery. Marland was trying to maneuver his big Parrott cannon off the field when several Texans came up and ordered him to the rear. Marland, seeing an opportunity for escape, charged the bridge with his eight horse team that was pulling the cannon. His lone charge across the bridge astonished the Texans on the bridge and caused them to jump for their lives off the bridge into the bayou, which allowed Marland to escape. As a result, Marland was given the Congressional Medal of Honor for bravery and he also had the honor of the bridge being named after him. All in all, there were 812 casualties, 124 wounded, and 566 missing after the battle was over. It was a total victory for the Confederates.

This historic bridge is also said to be the location of several body-dumpings during the 1950's and people have claimed to see one of these figures, known as the "lady in white", roaming around the bridge. There have also been reports of seeing large orange balls of light crossing the bridge. I had read several books that mentioned this bridge and was quite eager to pay it a visit. When we arrived, I was surprised to see a fairly modern looking concrete bridge. Over the years, it had been reconstructed from its original wooden frame into its current concrete structure. We simply walked around taking a few pictures, talking about the history of the area. Being it was the middle of September; mosquitoes were in their prime and were starting to feast. After losing about a pint of blood, we decided to leave. Before we went our different ways, the group's case manager asked me if I had ever heard of Chretian Point Plantation. Not familiar with the location, he proceeded to tell me a little of its history. He also said that it was within a mile of the bridge and asked me if I wanted to see it.

Chretian Point is a beautiful plantation home located in Sunset. For you movie buff's out there; the famous staircase descended by Scarlett O'Hara in "Gone with the Wind" is modeled after the main staircase of Chretian Point. Built by Hypolite Chretian II in 1831 on a 1776 Spanish land grant, the home has a long and dark history. Hypolite II later died, leaving the property to his wife, Felicite Chretian. Felecite, a Spaniard, was quite an interesting individual. Standing only four feet, ten inches, Felicite ran an entire plantation, smoked cigars, managed her servants, and is said to have regularly worn slacks, which was unheard of for a woman of that time.

Felicite is most infamously known for an incident involving one of Jean Lafitte's fellow pirates. The area of Sunset, Louisiana, and below is historically known for being a portion of the state often patrolled by Lafitte and his men. Often portrayed as a negative entity, Lafitte and his army of three thousand men, played a huge role in assisting Andrew Jackson in defending Louisiana against the British during the Battle of New Orleans in 1815. However, once Lafitte escaped to his hideaway in Galveston, Texas, many of his marauders lingered behind to pillage and rob the local homes. On one particular night, one of these pirates made his way to the porch of Felicite Chretian, with the hopes of robbing the house of its belongings. It is quite the understatement to say that the pirate underestimated the small stature of Felicite. As he approached the home with the attempts of demanding money and goods, he was fatally shot on the porch by Felicite. With the help of her loyal servants, they carried the body to the rear of the property and disposed of it in a small pond.

As several years passed, Felecite moved to New Orleans and turned over the control of the land to her son, Hypolite III. In 1863, Hypolite III successfully protected the house from being destroyed by Union troops. Several skirmishes took place on the actual front yard of the home; leading to the major battle mentioned earlier on the banks of Bayou Bourbeau. During one of these skirmishes, Union soldiers were firing over the home onto the Confederates. Several of these shots went astray, lodging themselves into the home and the large oak trees in the front yard. In an attempt to save the house from destruction, Hypolite III made his way to the second-story balcony, giving the Masonic distress signal. Fortunately, the Union leader, General Nathaniel Banks, who was also a Mason, returned the signal and agreed to spare the house. Despite the save, Union troops still reportedly made off with supplies and equipment said to be worth over $60,000.

For years, the plantation has said to have numerous paranormal events that have taken place. It is unsure as to whether the home is either haunted by the murdered pirate, Ms. Felicite herself, or a combination of both. Regardless, the place was extremely beautiful, as we pulled into its long driveway, adorned with numerous oak trees, which looked to be several hundred years old. We exited our vehicles and took several pictures of the outside while we discussed the home's illustrious history. After a few minutes of walking the grounds I felt something brush my face, only to find it was a spider web. I looked up and saw the largest spider web I have ever seen in my life connecting from the ground to the first branch of the oak tree. The web was literally about ten feet in circumference, which was an amazing, yet terrifying site. In the center of the web was one of those damn banana spiders that were literally about seven to eight inches long. Just as I began to back up, I realized that this spider was not alone. Every one of the massive oak trees contained these gigantic webs, literally infested with these mammoth freaking spiders. My ridiculously severe arachnophobia quickly kicked it and I knew it was time to leave.

After returning from my Sunset visit, I continued talking with the members on the LGH message board until I finally received a call from one of the founders. As with the other members I had already spoke with, I expressed my immense interest for joining, especially after the few outings I had already made. At the time, the group mainly covered the areas in and around Lafayette and Baton Rouge. Being I was from Central Louisiana, I felt that I had a lot to offer to the group, as I would be able to assist them in expanding their coverage area further north. The founder agreed and said she would consider not only bringing me in the group, but she was going to entertain the idea of making me a case manager. It doesn't seem like much, but at the time, due to my passion for the hobby, I really thought it was a big deal.

Although I was not an official member just yet, I was pushing the boards hard, paving the way for my entrance. One day I checked my e-mail and received a message from a woman in Leesville, Louisiana, named Jamie Jones. Apparently Jamie had assumed that I was a member of the group due to my activeness on the message boards. Jamie was actually coming to me with the claims that her house was haunted and she was terrified to stay there. Desperately in need of help, she turned to me, of all people. My first legitimate investigation and I wasn't even an actual member yet.

7

THE JONES'S RESIDENCE (LEESVILLE, LA)

I had absolutely no idea where I needed to start. In the several e-mails we had exchanged, it was obvious that Jamie felt there were strange things taking place at her home and needed some sort of guidance. However, I had never dealt with the investigation of a private residence and did not want to come off as seeming unprofessional. I have found this to be the hardest transition for paranormal groups just starting out. The initial switch from solely investigating cemeteries to investigating private homes is a drastic change. Now you are dealing with real people and real emotions, not to mention liability issues if injuries were to accrue. The homeowners are taking a huge gamble by just speaking out to look for help, much less having enough trust in allowing a group of strangers into their home to conduct an investigation. This is why it is a necessity that the team offers the best possible services possible, in the most professional of manners.

I decided that I would simply call Jamie and conduct an interview over the phone, documenting everything that she said. As we spoke, I definitely noticed a sort of anxiousness in her voice. Being an already naturally-excited individual, Jamie could not finish a sentence, as she had so many experiences to tell, she would quickly begin telling another story before she was finished with the first one.

From our first conversation I had learned that the property consisted of three homes: a trailer that Jamie and her husband, Danny, lived in, another trailer that was abandoned, and a larger abandoned home that was built off the ground. What I was told next sounded like something that came straight from a daytime talk show. The original main house that was on the property had belonged to Danny and his first wife. The now abandoned trailer belonged to Danny's aunt, who died on the kitchen floor of a heart attack. During this tough time, things became tougher, as Danny's marriage began to crumble. Once separated, Danny then began to have a relationship with Jamie. Obviously, this infuriated the ex-wife, as she despised seeing the two together. After a while of being together, the talks of remarriage were abound, as Danny's ex-wife stated on numerous occasions that she would see to it that the two never got married. Despite the strong interference, Danny and Jamie married, moving the currently inhabited trailer onto the property. A few years went by, yet the intense animosity was alive and well. Fate seemed to play another cruel trick, for as Danny's ex-wife was eight months pregnant for another individual, she suddenly died as well. Although she didn't die on the property, Jamie tremendously felt that the activity she was experiencing was caused by the ex-wife.

As I mentioned earlier, an individual does not have to necessarily die in a specific location in order for it to be haunted by them. In many cases, all it takes is for the individual to have strong emotional ties to the location for their spirit to return there. It is safe to say that there was plenty of emotion present in this situation, especially since she was so far into her pregnancy when she passed.

I then proceeded to question Jamie in regards to the types of activity she was experiencing. She started out by saying that the events were solely experienced by her and her young daughter. Danny had experienced absolutely nothing and was beginning to think Jamie was literally crazy. However, it felt very real to Jamie, as she felt so tormented; she now refused to sleep in her own bedroom, camping out on her living room floor every night. The activity began very mildly at first; with Jamie initially hearing disembodied footsteps coming down the hallway. Things then started to intensify as Jamie now started to hear people talking in the other room, seeing shadows in the corner of her eyes, and the feeling of being watched. After more and more strange events took place, she was almost positive that most of the activity was due to the deceased ex-wife. In one particular incident, Jamie and Danny's wedding picture literally flew off the wall. At this point, Jamie was nearly a nervous wreck and was in need of some assistance.

I knew something had to be done, but what could I do? I was still in the process of trying to get in a group that seemed like it would have been easier to be selected as the next Pope. I then returned to the LGH message board to discuss the information that was given to me by Jamie. I went into detail with all of the activity that was reported as well as the history of the residences. Low and behold, I started getting response after response. Now that I had an investigation, people wanted to start talking with me. Something should have clicked in my head that something wasn't right, yet my intense desire to be on what I thought was a legitimate team, caused me to overlook the bad vibes I was picking up.

During our conversations, Jamie had expressed wanting me to pay her a visit and conduct a preliminary, which pretty much consisted of taking photographs, audio recordings, and conducting EMF sweeps. Apparently, Jamie must have assumed that I had a little more experience under my belt than I actually had, yet I could not stand to tell her that I had actually never conducted a real investigation. I hoped that with my years of research and my general people skills, I could basically wing it. I quickly ran to the local electronics store and bought a thirty dollar voice recorder to accompany my small arsenal which consisted of a digital camera and a K-II meter. I then decided to bring my friend, Dustyn, simply for back up. After all, I really didn't know these people and didn't want to stumble upon the Manson family.

We arrived at the residence with quite a surprise. When people initially think of a haunted house in Louisiana, they usually have the stereotypical preconception of a huge plantation home with large Doric or Corinthian columns, ordaining the front. However, this was not quite the case here. As reported, the land consisted of two mobile homes and an older home built off of the ground. We exited the vehicle and were promptly greeted by a very excited Jamie, who was accompanied by her mom. It was obvious that Jamie was so glad we were there because she instantly began talking about the different things she has had happen at the home. To this day, I'm not sure if she was glad we were there to possibly help or just the simple fact that we were there to listen to her claims. In many cases, a simple reassurance for the homeowner is all they need so they don't feel that they are crazy.

After listening to several more stories from Jamie and her mom, we were taken through the homes to look around. First, we went into Jamie's trailer, where a majority of the events take place. We were in the hallway, near her bedroom, as Jamie was telling us about an incident that had happened the night before. As she was talking, I could have sworn that I heard a female's voice coming from the bedroom. I walked in the room, only to find that no one was in there. Still, I said to myself that it was probably just my mind playing tricks on me, especially since it was the first time I was doing something like this. We then made our way to the older house that Danny and his ex-wife used to live in. We were accompanied by Jamie's dog, which, as we went to enter, he began to whimper and walk backwards out of the house. As with young children, pets are also said to have an enhanced sixth sense in regards to paranormal phenomena.

Due to the fact that it was only 1:00 PM, we decided that we would place a voice recorder in the old house, lock the door, and the four of us would leave the property, leaving the house completely unattended. After lunch, we returned to retrieve the recorder and hear a few more of Jamie's stories. I mentioned to her about the possibilities of bringing LGH to investigate, in which she was quite receptive to the idea. Before we said our goodbyes, I asked Jamie to see if she could visit the local court house and try to find as much information that she could on the history of the land. I then headed home, looking forward to going over my very first audio recordings. Who would have imagined I would actually get something in the middle of the day.

Getting your first EVP is truly a unique thing. Luckily, I obtained mine a little sooner than normal, as it was my very attempt. There is nothing creepier than sitting in a dark and quiet room, listening to a constant hiss on your headphones until you suddenly hear something that is unexplainable. This was the case after my visit to Jamie's. After about thirty minutes of quiet audio, I captured a female voice saying, "Danny." What made it more credible was the fact that no one was anywhere on the property when this unknown voice was captured. Also, this was the name of the homeowner. Could this have been caused by the deceased ex-wife rumored to haunt the grounds? No one was quite sure, yet it truly was amazing to record the voice of an unknown female calling the name of the current homeowner while it was verified that no one was present at the time.

I then took the audio recording to Jamie to get her opinion, which she was quite impressed, yet concerned, with it. What was additionally interesting was the history on the property that was recovered from the courthouse. The land was located in a narrow strip near the Texas border that was once called "No Man's Land." It received its name due to the fact that in the 1800's, this portion of the Louisiana-Texas border was under no legal jurisdiction from any law enforcement agency. Due to this, the land was literally a hideout for criminals that were fleeing from the law, seeking amnesty. One can only imagine what type of people this area became home to, as well as what additional crimes were committed here.

Upon further research on the property, which was actually a much larger piece of land than we expected, it was discovered that it once belonged to the original district judge of Vernon Parish, Nathan M. Bray. In the area that was now wooded, stood the home of Mr. Bray, who was considered a very prominent man at the time. On one quiet night, two unknown individuals approached the property and brutally stabbed Mr. Bray to death. No one was ever apprehended for the murder and it is still unknown as to the motives behind the crime. Whether it was an attempted burglary gone wrong or a couple of criminals that were seeking retribution for a harsh sentence they were once given by the judge, no one will ever know.

With such an interesting past that included, murder, natural deaths, and breeding grounds for fleeing felons, one could only fathom the amount of negative energy lingering around. Considering the additional fact that I had obtained such an interesting audio recording, I felt that the area could have been haunted by more than one spirit. On numerous occasions, Jamie did report feeling the presence of more than one entity. Although I didn't have any experience in the investigation field, I knew that with the history involved and the concern of Jamie, some sort of formal investigation was warranted.

I returned to the LGH boards with my report including the history, list of strange occurrences, and the interesting EVP that I had captured. Unsurprisingly, everyone wanted to talk to me now, saying that they definitely wanted to investigate the homes. It was at this time that I was pretty much welcomed into the group by the "powers that be." Several years after, I would learn that I was accused of attempting to "steal" the Jones's investigation and I was basically only let in the group because I could get them access to the residence. How pathetic is that? First off, where in the hell was I going to take the investigation if I would have "stolen" it? Second, what gives copyrights to a location to make someone think that it belongs to them anyway? This territorial persona will be discussed many more times throughout this book, as this is an ongoing problem with many groups across the country.

Despite the issues that would plague me later, for the moment, I was elated that I was now part of a paranormal investigative team. My first actual investigation would be, of course, the Jones's residence. The first thing that I wanted to do as a member was obtain more equipment, specifically a CCTV surveillance system. At the time, the group was not very equipped; only having two handheld video cameras, a few EMF meters, and two or three voice recorders. From what I had learned from Steve, most of the group did not rely on concrete evidence to validate that a place was active. Unfortunately, they would base a majority of their results on one of the members who claimed to be sensitive. I had no issues with people using sensitives as one of their investigative tools, yet for my own self-reassurance, I still needed some type of hard evidence to make me believe, as well as to validate to the client that we had found something of interest.

One of my worst vices is that I am an extremely compulsive buyer. If I have, so much as the slightest urge to buy something, I will act on a whim and get it, which was the case with the DVR system that I wanted. I grabbed for my credit card, which was already in bad shape, and finished it off for good. I initially purchased four IR cameras and a quad processor. The DVR was cleverly acquired a week later, when I found one on sale at the department store. I quickly called my wife and said, "Hey they have a real nice DVR for sale. Wouldn't that be nice so you could record all of your favorite shows while you are working?" With that slick maneuver, I now had a complete surveillance system and was ready to kick ass and take names.

The investigation date was set for a Saturday evening. I was to meet the entire group in Alexandria and take them to Jamie's, which was about an hour away. Leading up to that weekend, I was extremely anxious to not only conduct an actual investigation, but to try out my new equipment. The team already had their pre-designed LGH shirts, so I had to rush and find one that was compatible. After getting a five dollar t-shirt, I ironed on some white letters, spelling out "LGH".

Looking back, that was the cheesiest stuff I ever did, yet at the time, I was quite proud to adorn my cheap t-shirt with my crooked stencil iron-on letters.

I have always been the type of person who is shy of meeting new people. So was the case here, as I was extremely nervous to meet the group, as I wanted to make a good impression. After waiting a while at a pre-determined meeting spot, the group arrived. A total of six members showed up, including Steve, who had now made it back from his tour of duty in New Orleans. Another member present was Elissa, who is still in the group with me to this day. Elissa is a great person who has shown her dedication time and time again and I am very happy to have met her that evening. As far as some of the others present that night; I had my doubts.

One member stood there in a in a fetal-like position, appearing as though he would jump every time a bird would chirp. For namesake purposes, I will simply call him "Mr. Personality". He dressed in dark clothes, an army jacket, and what looked like a fisherman's hat, minus the bait. He simply radiated a coldness that I did not quite have the time or patience to deal with. Still, being the nice person I am, I approached him and introduced myself. As I extended my hand, he looked at it and turned the other way. Can you imagine the nerve of this person. I then introduced myself to the others who were somewhat friendly. However, the only two that were really nice were Steve and Elissa. As I looked around at the members, I noticed that one was missing. I was then told that she was sitting in the car because she was feeling ill. When I asked what was wrong, I was told that she was the sensitive member of the group and, even though we were still an hour away from Jamie's, she felt such negative energy from the place, she felt ill. Honestly, I didn't know what to think at the time, but if I knew then what I know now, I would have probably got back in my truck and turned around. I was now in a group that a majority of the members were not very welcoming of my arrival. Still, I put all the awkwardness in the back of my head and proceeded to lead everyone to Jamie's.

We arrived at the home around 7:00 PM. I introduced everyone to Jamie and began to show them around the property, showing them the specific locations where strange occurrences had taken place. I then noticed the "sensitive" member and Mr. Personality walk off by themselves. When I asked what they were doing, I was told that it was a tradition of the two to walk around the property alone, so she could get a "feel" for the place. Of course, the meager Mr. Personality was following in toe, supposedly validating everything she was claiming to feel, as he too, claimed to have sensitive abilities.

We then began to setup the IR cameras throughout two of the three homes, connecting them to the DVR, enabling us to monitor several areas at once. Being this was my first investigation, I simply wanted to lay low and follow everyone's lead. As with investigation, we had to group up in pairs of two. We do this not only for safety reasons, but for validation purposes as well. My partner for the night was Steve, as I felt most comfortable with him. We made our way to the original old house to begin our investigation.

There are various styles that people use to conduct an investigation. Some like to walk around with a video camera, documenting every moment of the night. Others snap hundreds of pictures while taking EMF readings and audio samples. My favorite technique is to simply find a place to sit quietly, relax, and get a feel for the area. We would initially take this approach, as we set up chairs in what was once the living room, placing them against the wall. We sat there in total darkness. It was at this point that it hit me; I was now a paranormal investigator. I was now doing the very same things I had religiously watched others do every week on television. There was not a sound to be heard or a thing to see in the dark, yet I was having the time of my life.

Steve and I continued to sit motionless in the home, only moving to take an occasional photograph. The one thing about sitting in a completely dark area for long periods of time, is that your other senses become extremely fine-tuned, especially your hearing. The slightest sound seemed to be much louder, regardless of where it is coming from. After a while of sitting quietly, we naturally became a little bored and began talking with one another. As we spoke, we began to hear what sounded like two people talking down the hallways in one of the bedrooms. We knew no one else was in the house so we quickly quieted down to focus on the voices. The voices were vague and we could not decipher what was being said, but it was definitely apparent that a conversation was being had. Even though I started to get a little freaked out, I wanted to go and find out where these voices were coming from, yet I didn't want to scare anything away. I guess it is that nervous rush that makes paranormal investigating so enjoyable. Although you are scared at the time, you are left with a rush of adrenaline, leaving you wanting more.

We continued to sit there quietly, focusing on these unknown voices. I closed my eyes and sat back in my chair, trying to concentrate on what was being said. I don't know if it was because I was concentrating more or what, but it seemed as if the voices were getting closer and closer. As the voices grew louder, I began to feel a vibration in the floor. Keep in mind that the house was built off the ground, so you could feel any movement on the floor. The rhythm of the vibrations was exactly the same as if someone was walking down the hallway. However, as I said, we were completely alone in the house. The footsteps started very soft at first and then began to get much more intense, as if whatever was causing these steps was getting closer. The vibrations would radiate through the floor, into my feet, and up to my legs. As I turned to Steve, the two of us didn't have to say a word, as we knew what each other were thinking. The footsteps grew so close; they felt like they were about twenty feet away. It took everything in my powers not to turn on my flashlight, as this was about the most intense experience I had ever had to this point of my short investigating career. Instead, I reached for my camera and slowly pointed it in the direction that the sounds were coming from. It was as if I was deer hunting; I didn't want to make any sudden movements, as I did not want to scare anything away. I quickly snapped a picture with the hopes of capturing the source of these strange noises. What the picture captured shocked me, as I had a large black, shadowed obstruction right in the center of the picture. The anomaly appeared to be about twenty feet in front of me, validating the proximity of the footsteps we were hearing. To this day, that experience involving the footsteps, voices, and shadow will remain one of my most intense experiences as an investigator. I guess that is why I have liked the Jones's residence so much; it has been a place of many paranormal first for me. People are often surprised when they ask me what is one of the most locally haunted places I have visited and I tell them about Jamie's.

After such a strange encounter, it took Steve and I a while to regain our composure, as we still couldn't believe what we had experienced. Once we did, we decided to rotate to Jamie's house and allow other investigators the chance to investigate the old house. Everyone was amazed when they heard our experience so they quickly went to try their luck with the strange sounds and footsteps. Unfortunately, we were the only ones who had that type of experience during the night.

Jamie was getting extremely excited that she was finally getting some validation to her experiences. She now knew that she wasn't crazy and had others who had experienced things on her property as well. Seeing how much emotion was involved in this family regarding the possibilities that the house may be haunted by Danny's ex-wife, I came up with the idea that Jamie should get involved with the investigation. It only seemed right to have Jamie to assist, since it seemed that a majority of the occurrences focused around her anyways.

At this point, I had now paired up with Elissa and we took Jamie to her bedroom, which is where she had reported most of the activity. I placed a voice recorder on her nightstand and quietly sat on her bed, holding an EMF meter. I then instructed Jamie to simply ask questions aloud, inquiring as to why this presence was in her home. After several minutes of doing this, nothing out the ordinary was happening. Jamie then began to ask very personal questions regarding the ex-wife and her resentment of Danny and Jamie's wedding. Almost immediately after doing this, I began to get very large and consistent spikes on the meter. I could not believe that my idea worked, as it seemed that we were hitting a nerve with such specific questions. As the readings on the meter began to dissipate, I stood up from the bed. It seemed as though I had re-captured this unusual pocket of EMF energy, as the meter was set off again. We then began what seemed like a game of hide and seek; the readings on the meter would lessen until I would catch back up with it, proving that whatever was in the room with us was actually moving around. The wild goose chase led me completely around the bedroom until I eventually ran straight into Jamie. When I did, Jamie remarked that she felt an electrostatic charge, causing the hair on her arms to stand straight up. Then, as suddenly as the activity started, it vanished.

From the living room, which was where the DVR monitoring station was set up, I began to hear high pitched squealing and yelling. I briskly walked to the living room to see what the commotion was all about. There I found the sensitive member of the group and Mr. Personality staring at the monitor in awe, as they screamed that the camera was picking up hundreds of orbs. After looking at the screen, I quickly informed them that the orbs they were clucking at were simply particles of dust that were kicked up from our presence in the bedroom. I then gave them a brief lesson on how IR cameras worked and how certain things, such as dust, were much more visible than on a regular camera. Immediately, I could feel the negative vibes from the two, who I'm sure were saying, "Who does this rookie think he is?" The sensitive member, who we will go ahead and call "Becky", then decided that it was time for her and Mr. Personality to have their shot with Jamie in the bedroom, solely on a paranormal basis, of course.

I swear, the two were not in the room five minutes before they came limping back, as if they had returned from a battle. Becky was holding her back while Mr. Personality was literally carrying her back to the living room. It seemed as though Becky had claimed to have come in contact with a black male spirit and he did not want us to be there. What came next shocked me; as Becky crawled into the fetal position on Jamie's couch, said that the spirit had drained her of her energy, and then fell asleep. I know I may have been the rookie of the group, but I didn't have to have a Doctorate in Parapsychology to see that was not how you were supposed to conduct an investigation, especially of someone's private residence. Still, being the rookie, I never said a word and proceeded to investigate in the fashion that I had been doing. We went on for about another hour before we decided to call it a night. After we packed up our gear, we woke up Becky (yes, she was still sleeping), and we headed back home.

Despite the fact that some of the members investigated in a manner that I did not fully agree with, I had the time of my life, as I had officially conducted my first investigation with, what was, at the time, a legitimate group. I returned home with the daunting task of going over all the audio and video. Video proved to yield nothing substantial on this visit, as I was quickly introduced to the frustration of using IR cameras in a dusty house. Audio, however, produced some interesting results from the bedroom when no one was in there. A strange growl was captured that didn't sound like any of the group members. In another recording, when I asked if whoever was there had earlier said, "Help me" from a previous recording, you can hear a second voice clearly say, "Help." It was as if whoever was there was answering my question by mocking me.

Jamie and her family were very pleased with the results we had found from the first investigation. After we educated her on what was taking place in her home, she no longer lived in fear. She moved her mattress back to its suitable location and, for the first time in years, she actually slept in her own bedroom. Her hauntings then began to be a daily part of her life as her and her family began to joke about it, which is something that would not have even been thought of prior to our visits. Her new found passion for the paranormal even caused her and some of her friends to form a small ghost hunting group. Speaking in regards to a woman who was once too terrified to sleep in her own bedroom; this was a huge accomplishment. It was from this point on; I became deeply dedicated to educating others in the many facets of the paranormal. Many times, all it takes is a friendly ear to reassure someone that they are not crazy and teach them how to handle certain occurrences.

I have always been a firm believer in follow-up investigations. I personally feel that no matter how haunted a place may be, it does not contain activity every night of the week. Unfortunately, we don't have contracts with spirits and we cannot make them act on command. If I could, I sure could make one hell of an awesome haunted house and charge people to investigate it. Oh wait, I think there are actually people around that do that very same thing. The only difference is that the place is rigged with special effects so you have no clue what is staged and what isn't. It's amazing what people will do for a little notoriety, yet it is even more shocking that people fall for it, which takes me back to my whole "a sucker is born every day" speech I gave earlier.

It wasn't until nearly a year later, I would return to the Jones's residence with the same California film crew I mentioned from Ft. Derussy. We would conduct another full investigation of the property, placing IR cameras throughout the three homes. As with the previous visit, we encouraged Jamie to partake in the investigation, hoping that her presence would spark some activity. Again, things did not start to happen until Jamie began asking personal questions, directed to the ex-wife. In one incident, Jamie asked, "Do you know that you've died?" Immediately after she asked this, we received a very strong EMF spike. Keep in mind that this took place in the abandoned trailer, which had no electricity connected to it. This happened several other times throughout the night, which astonished the film crew.

As mentioned, IR cameras were strewn throughout the three homes. Steve was assigned to monitoring the cameras that were in the old house. Steve, who smokes like a damn train, took a break for one of his many smoke breaks. When he returned to the monitoring station, he noticed that one of the bedroom doors was not in the position that it was in earlier. One of the best things about a DVR system is that you can simultaneously review recorded video while continuing to record new one. After rewinding the video, we were amazed to see the door actually close on its own. There were no open windows in the room and no drafts presents that could have moved the door. When we attempted to recreate the door closing on its own, we found it to be very back-heavy, meaning that when we would close the door, it would swing back open. In the video, the door closed about half way and then stayed in that same position. Upon further reviewing of the video, I also noticed that just prior to the door moving, you could see some sort of white mist near the bottom corner of the door. It quickly appears and fades, just as the door is set in motion. It was almost as if this unknown mist was the energy that moved the door. Needless to say, everyone was freaking out over the video clip. Once complete, it would be discovered that we would catch the door closing even more a few hours later. In this instance, there was no mist caught prior to the door moving, however we did capture a strange array of what looked like confetti, quickly fly across the screen. Seconds after, the door moved. In both cases, prior to the door closing, there was some sort of strange activity captured, whether it was a mist or orb-like activity.

On a personal note, I would like deeply thank Jamie and her family for not only making that initial contact with me, but for also having the trust to allow us in their home on numerous occasions. Throughout the years, I would investigate many more private residences, yet none would contain as much personal emotion and activity as the Jones's residence. Unfortunately, I do not keep in touch with the Jones's as often as I would like but I want them to know that they were definitely a catalyst for keeping my interest sparked in continuing my hobby, which can often be boring for most at the beginning. Many people start investigating, not realizing that it can often get very boring. After several uneventful investigations, they quickly lose interest and quit the hobby all together. Luckily for me, my first investigation was the Jones's and it definitely had the ambience that I needed to keep the ball rolling. Unfortunately, not all investigations would be this eventful, as I soon would find out that there are some strange individuals in the paranormal community. Despite the quirks with LGH, I blew them off and anxiously anticipated the next investigation. Little did I know the type of people I was going to start to meet and the real headache behind a paranormal investigative group.

8
INTERESTING CHARACTERS

Let's face it, there are some stupid people on this planet. My grandmother used to refer to someone like this as "not being the one who grated the moon to make the stars." Personally, I have zero tolerance for people who are just plain stupid and I usually don't mind telling them. Needless to say, I had already experienced my share of stupidity, especially when working in law enforcement for so long. I truly felt that our prison system was one of the many breeding grounds for stupidity, as the people who are in there are not quite the brightest people around. After all, they got caught didn't they?

It would soon become apparent to me that my patience for dim-witted people was going to be tested as I dealt with more and more individuals in the paranormal. It is safe to say that amongst the thousands of paranormal groups in existence, there contains some of the widest varieties of personalities one can imagine. There may be a group that only has ten members, yet their personalities range from everything from a seventy year old scientist to an eighteen year old devil worshiper. This causes an extremely varied melting pot that could boil over with tensions at any given time. These varied personalities do not only apply for the members, as it also carries over to the actual clients who contact us. I would have to say that about 70 percent of those who contact us are legitimately concerned individuals who live normal lives and are genuinely frightened by what is taking place in their homes. The others make up a combination of eccentric individuals who have it so set in their mind that their house is haunted, nothing you can prove to them will change their minds. Others are simply lonely and wanting some attention. This often comes with single, elderly women, who just want someone to speak with. The group that I like the least is the ones who intentionally fake evidence at their residence simply to be noticed or business owners wanting to boost business. I call this the "Amityville Syndrome" as their actions strongly resemble those of the infamous George Lutz.

Horror movie buffs like myself are all quite familiar with the murders that took place on November 13, 1974, at 112 Ocean Avenue in Amityville, New York. On this night, Ronald DeFeo, Jr. murdered his father, mother, two brothers, and two sisters. Upon questioning, DeFeo claimed that he committed the murders due to demonic voices in his head that told him to do so. The home was then bought by George and Kathy Lutz, who immediately began claiming that the house was extremely haunted, inspiring some of the most notorious media coverage around. Their short stay of only twenty-eight days reportedly consisted of some of the most horrific and demonic-like hauntings ever experienced. It was not until just prior to George's death in May of 2006, did he finally come clean, admitting that all of the haunted accounts had been falsified in an attempt to get out of a home mortgage that he could not afford.

I never quite could understand how someone would go to such extremes as to want to make false claims of their house being haunted. What is even worse is dealing with clients who will purposely fake evidence to strengthen their claims. The founder of one group told me of a residence that they investigated where the homeowner reported hearing strange voices in their house. Upon further investigating, it was discovered that the homeowner had painstakingly embedded a speaker in their wall, resulting in sounds and voices radiating from an unknown origin. I'm sorry, but this ticks me off to no end. We, as hobbyist, are already at a disadvantage because we do this completely free of charge. We take the time away from our families and jobs and drive hundreds of miles, all at our own expenses, only to find out that all of our work was a complete waste of time. The simple concept of that act of selfishness made me irate, even though it had never happened to me; up to this point.

It had only been several weeks since my first investigation at Jamie's and things were going pretty well. I was starting to get comfortable with the group, making a few more friends along the way. One of the investigators from the Baton Rouge area had obtained an investigation from a small town near New Orleans. The homeowner was a single mother of a teenage son and a young daughter. Her and her family lived in a home where an elderly woman was bludgeoned to death by her adult grandson. The man was now serving a life sentence for the murder, although he claimed that it was due to hearing demonic voices in his head (sounds familiar.).

The current homeowner was quite concerned, as her young daughter was in fear of an elderly man that she claimed to often see in her window at night. According to the mother, the teenage son was of little help, as he often antagonized the sister and frightened her even more regarding this elderly male. We agreed that we would conduct an investigation of the residence, especially since a young child was involved.

Being I was from central Louisiana, I had the farthest to drive, which was a little over three hours. With gasoline costing more than a gallon of milk, the drive alone, would result in an expensive trip. The drive was quite interesting, as the town had been heavily hit from Hurricane Katrina. Even though it was about four months after the hurricane, the devastation and debris were still abundant. I am not exaggerating when I say that as I drove, there were piles of debris approximately twenty feet high every fifty feet. These mounds of broken homes and trees went for miles, as the cleanup process had begun.

We arrived at the residence, which was literally in B.F. Egypt, meeting with the homeowner and her teenage son. Immediately, her son acted in a strange manner however, we still had a job to do, so we set up all of our surveillance equipment and began to conduct the investigation. The night went pretty uneventful for several hours. Everyone took a break, as the homeowner had graciously provided snacks for us. When we returned to the monitors, we noticed that the back door was opened. As with the Jones's residence, we reviewed the video to catch the exact point that the door moved.

What we saw next infuriated us, as you could plainly see the teenage son run across the screen after he opened the door from the outside. What the idiot failed to realize was that we were using IR cameras, which could see in total darkness and easily captured him in the picture, despite the fact that he even had the gall to change shirts prior to his antics. What was even more ridiculous was that the kid opened the door and ran in the direction that it opened. He could of at least ran around the house so no one could have seen him, but I suppose that is how idiots operate.

As soon as we saw this we immediately stopped the investigation. Anytime we find tainted evidence, we must throw out anything else captured during the night, as we are unsure what is real and what is staged. When we told the homeowner about this and showed her the video, she burst into tears, ashamed of what her son had done. I honestly felt bad for her, as I truly feel she was genuinely frightened for her and her daughter. Whether or not there was something unknown taking place at the home, we are still unsure, yet due to the boy's unnecessary behavior, everything was unfortunately dismissed. Then again, despite all the theatrics, there must have been some sort of spirit present because Becky and Mr. Personality still picked up on an old man that was haunting the residence. Please keep in mind that I said that with total sarcasm. As I made the long drive home, I couldn't help but remain pissed as my time and money had now been wasted.

A few weeks had passed and we now began to make lightly of that unfortunate investigation. We had now received a new member in the group, who was from northern Louisiana, which added even more coverage of the state. This individual claimed to have operated a small production company and wanted to make a documentary on the group's investigations. As with me being brought in because I had an investigation to offer, I am pretty sure this member was solely brought in due to her media capabilities. In addition, this member brought to the table an investigation, which was of an art museum in Monroe, which proved to be one hell of an event.

As the days before the investigation approached, we all became extremely excited. This was our first investigation of a known public establishment and we were going to have media coverage from the local newspaper. In addition, the new member said that her film crew was going to be present to begin the making of the documentary. She was hyping up the event for all of us, stating that the news of our arrival had leaked out to the public and they were expecting a crowd to be present. She went to say that because of this, she would now have security present to keep the onlookers at bay. Man, I couldn't believe this. Not only was I investigating with a group that was on national television, but we would now have security to keep the public away. For a second, I almost felt famous. Needless to say, I would soon be reminded of the saying: "All that glitters is not gold."

At the time, there was not much known history on the museum other than a few visitors claimed to have to have an uneasy feeling when they visited the building. Being I was still new, it didn't matter to me. I simply packed up my equipment and went where the group leaders said to go. We were all extremely excited about the investigation, as the hype of stardom continued to be pumped through our veins. Driving up there, my mind began to run wildly, imagining hordes of people being held back by security, just to get a glimpse of the team, as roses and bras rained from the heavens.

As we entered Monroe, I could hardly even keep still, having no clue what we were going to experience. I did not quite know the exact location of the museum, yet I figured I would just drive until I saw a huge group of people cheering our name. As we approached the street that the museum was located on, I passed up a large building where I saw the new group member waiving us down. We had finally made it to the museum, however there was one problem; there was no one there. Where were the crowds of people dropping to their feet at our mere presence? Where was the security? Most importantly, where was this professional production company?

We exited our vehicles to formerly meet our newest member. I could not help but immediately notice that she was wearing a t-shirt that had the name of her "production company" airbrushed on the back of it. Yes, you heard me right: airbrushed. She then proceeded to say that her production team was inside taking still shots. Just as she said that, her "team" made their way out to meet us. The team that she so diligently mentioned actually consisted of her mom and dad, who both had, of course, the same airbrushed t-shirts, spreading the production propaganda. At this point, it was taking everything inside for me to keep my composure. I was holding up pretty well until the father turned around and I noticed that on his back, in addition to the production company's name, it also said, "Security." Keep in mind that this poor man looked like he was about sixty-five years old. Was this going to be the security that was supposedly going to insure our safety when these hordes of people were supposed to flock to our feet? As soon as I saw that, I couldn't hold back any longer, as I burst out into laughter. Unfortunately, I have always been the type of person that could find humor out of anything. It is like a kid trying to keep from laughing in church; the harder you try not to laugh, the more you want to. As I looked around at the empty parking lot, it was apparent that there would be no huge crowds, which was actually a good thing, due to the health status of our "security" that already looked like he had one foot in the grave.

I just couldn't imagine how someone could think that they were a legitimate business entity carrying themselves in such fashion. I have heard of "mom and pop" businesses before, but this was pushing things a little too far. By this point in the night, I was literally expecting to see our security guard's pager go off, then rip off his shirt, exposing a "towing service" shirt, then taking off to handle his other business. From this point on, all I could do was uncontrollably snicker while proceeding to set up all of the equipment.

Another new member present that night was a guy by the name of Todd Weaver. Todd had minor dealings with LGH in the past, yet he had run a small investigative group on his own in the Shreveport area. Todd was extremely quiet, yet seemed as though he was very goal-oriented. Personally, Todd initially came off as an arrogant prick and I will be the first to admit that I did not like him very much at first. I would soon find out that this was not the case at all, as Todd just takes some getting used to. Todd would eventually play a huge role in the continuation of my paranormal adventure and would soon become one of my best friends, but more on Todd later.

We were told that a member from the local newspaper was going to be present. Surprisingly, despite everything else that was exaggerated, a woman from the paper actually showed up. Unfortunately, the reporter was not of the highest caliber. The poor girl was so gullible, she would later ask me my profession, and when I told her I was a "male escort", she believed me and began to annotate it on her little notepad. Luckily, I stopped her before she took it to press; otherwise the whole city of Monroe would have assumed I was a paranormal prostitute. Apparently, the girl had absolutely no experience with the paranormal, as she proceeded to ask some of the dumbest questions I had ever heard. The question that I will remember for as long as I live was when she asked one of the members what did ghost eat for breakfast. It took everything in my powers not to interrupt and answer her question by saying, "Boo Berries and Ghost Toast of course." Despite the ridiculous antics of the reporter, I soon would learn that, no matter what, always treat the media with respect, as they can make you or break you. In this particular case, they would break us, as several of the members would be the cause for a horrible write-up.

The investigation began with Becky doing her traditional walk-through of the building. She started off by saying that she felt the presence of an older woman wearing a blue dress. Coincidentally, as soon as you walked in the museum, there was a large portrait of the original owner of the building when it used to be a private home. The portrait depicted an elderly woman clad in, you guessed it, a blue dress. The curator of the museum had brought her nine-year old son with her, something we do not necessarily condone. I have always been against children being present on investigations not only for the sanitation of evidence, but for safety reasons as well. Still, this was the curator's building and we were in no position to tell her who she could and couldn't have in attendance. If she wanted her son present, all we could do is deal with it and continue on with our usual investigation. Regardless, the kid posed no threat to the investigation and remained quiet the entire evening.

About two hours had passed in what was now becoming an extremely uneventful investigation. By this time, Becky had made her way to the adjacent carriage house and levee area, claiming that she was picking up on numerous rapes and murders. However, when questioned, the curator knew of no violent rapes or murders ever taking place on the grounds. During this time, I was at the monitoring station, viewing the cameras that were run through the museum and the carriage house. I noticed on the video that Mr. Personality was investigating the carriage house. Keep in mind that this was one of the most scared individuals I had ever met. This was the same guy that once asked me to escort him down a twenty foot hallway, just so he could retrieve a flashlight. Anyways, as I watched him, I could see that he was scared by the way he was methodically taking very slow steps through the dark carriage house, not wanting to come up on anything unexpected. Just when it looked like the poor boy was going to have an aneurism, he goes and steps on a sheet of bubble wrap that was lying on the floor. I never saw someone move so fast, as he literally bolted from the house in a pathetically embarrassing manner.

Just when we thought things couldn't get any worse during the night, it did. The group leaders made the mistake of asking the curator if she could have her young son go sit in the vehicle by himself at one in the morning. When asked why, she was told that the spirits did not want to make themselves present, for fear of scaring the child. Apparently, the curator had enough of the BS for the night, as did many of us; because she then said that it was time for the group to wrap up the investigation. By this point, I was not about to argue, as the night was a fiasco. I then began to pack up all of my equipment, not knowing that things were about to get much worse.

As word spread that the investigation was now terminated, our beloved "Production Company" was sitting on the steps of the carriage house. In a last ditch effort to prolong the investigation, the new member/film director, came barging into the museum saying that a manifestation was "about to occur." I guess this is now a good time to say that this individual also claimed to have sensitive abilities. I could literally see the eyes of the curator and reporter roll, as they could see through the theatrics. Still, to pacify the masses, everyone walked outside to the carriage house to see what the big deal was. The three-man film crew then began pointing at one of the windows of the carriage house as they screamed, "Look. Did you see that? There was a face in that window." When we all agreed that we did not see anything, they then almost became defensive saying, "Well, we know what we saw."

Several minutes later, we returned to pack up all of our equipment in preparation of the long drive home that proved to be such a wasteful trip. To make matters just a little worse, putting the final nail in the coffin, the father of the director comes running in yelling that his daughter was diabetic and now having a seizure in the back yard. Again, my gallow-humor, which often makes up for a lack of sympathy, soon kicked in, as I nonchalantly continued to pack up my gear. I was so ashamed of everything that had taken place that night, still in awe from everything. How could people act like that and expect to be taken seriously? We all quickly escaped the city of Monroe for fear of what the newspaper had in store for us the next morning. Still, the optimistic part of me hoped maybe the reporter would have a sympathetic bone in her body and look past all the theatrics of the night and see that some of us were trying to conduct ourselves in a professional manner. Boy, would I be in for a surprise, as I opened up the morning paper.

The paper had a lengthy article on the previous night's investigation. However, the article did not consist of a thorough explanation of our scientific approach; instead it heavily mentioned the antics of the two sensitive individuals. As I said, the media can break you, always proving that the pen is mightier that the sword. Especially when dealing with the paranormal, which is already a topic often looked at as being taboo by many; it is essential that you should paint the picture to the audience that you are simply a normal person with an interesting hobby. Although the topic may be unique, by showing that you use common sense and a logical approach to it, will prove to be successful with any media no matter what. To this day, we have been featured in dozens of television, radio, newspaper, and magazine articles, all of which have been portrayed in a very good light. It all boils down to how you carry yourself and the approach you take. If you radiate the image that you are an arrogant psychic with outlandish claims, then you must be prepared to deal with the repercussions of a horrible write up. It may not necessarily be because the reporter didn't like you or you were misquoted. Despite how much you may not want to admit it, it may simply be because you made yourself look like an idiot.

Needless to say, after the newspaper article came out, morale was at an all-time low. Some wanted to crawl under a rock and never be seen wearing an LGH shirt again, while others were quick to start pointing the fingers at one another for such a fiasco. What came next was a huge battle that would drag out for several months between the "production company" and the "powers that be". Members of the group were blamed for acting in such a ridiculous manner, causing for such a horrible write-up, while the film crew were blamed for making promises they did not keep. Personally, I could have cared less about the whole ordeal, as I paid them no mind. I really cannot give you more details on all of the endless banter, as

I never paid any attention to it. All I remember is that the group leaders ended up removing the film director from the group, claiming that she was using the private contact information of former clients to contact them and attempt to line up her own investigations.

This would be the start of what seemed to be an ongoing drama-filled soap opera. By this point, the group leaders now began to constantly argue with one another. One would claim that they were the true leader while the other did the same. This would go back and forth all the time, dragging all of us into the mix. I'm not exaggerating when I say that at least once every two weeks, the two would get into a power struggle. In an effort to flex their muscles, they would simply delete everyone's e-mail accounts and shut down the message board. It got to the point where it was happening so much, I would go to check my e-mail, only to find the account was deleted, and not thinking much of it. We were all getting sick of the bickering, the negative light some of the members were getting, and the non-professional approach to an investigation. However, we continued to deal with it all because we enjoyed the actual hobby so much and hoped that with time, it would all iron itself out.

In addition to faked evidence, wacky reporters, and convulsing film directors, we cannot forget about the good old fashion paranoid schizophrenic individuals that contact you for some of the strangest request you can imagine. These are not your average people that think their home is haunted; these are people of a much stranger nature, obviously suffering from some sort of mental illness. Although it is unfortunate, I cannot help but laugh at some of the ridiculous requests that I have received.

One of the first strange e-mails that I received was from an individual claiming that the government was monitoring her. She stated that the government had set up surveillance equipment all across her property and was monitoring her every move. I can remember in one part of her e-mail she said, "I must keep this message short as they are watching my every move and are probably reading this message as I type." Her request was that she wanted us to come in and set up our surveillance equipment so we could catch the government spying on her. She would then take the evidence we captured and use it so she could press charges against the government for "invasion of privacy". Surprisingly, I actually wrote her back saying that I don't think we could help her with her problem and that it would be best to contact some sort of security company.

Another memorable request was from a female reporting strange activity in her home. She stated that while she was in bed at night, she would be awoken to strange noises. When she would sit up in her bed, she would see small creatures, about eight inches tall, sitting on the foot of her bed. As crazy as that sounded, she proceeded to saying that these creatures held small lassos, using them to rope hamsters, which ran across her floor during the night. This was one of those cases where I didn't even bother to respond, as the possibilities of what else would be reported were literally endless.

Despite these asinine requests for investigations, none would stay in my mind as long as the "clock lady". I received an e-mail from a woman in northern Louisiana, claiming to have psychic abilities. This, in itself, was not strange, as I often have people write to discuss their abilities, since it is not always a topic that they can discuss to just anyone. However, this case was a little more unique, as the woman claimed that she was able to communicate with beings of a "higher plane of existence". She stated that the beings she spoke with referred to themselves as "Joseph", "St. Michael the Archangel", as well as other hierarchies of God. Just when I thought it couldn't get any stranger, she proceeded to say that the method she was use to communicate with these beings was by means of a "Westclox alarm clock". I'm sorry, but how in the hell can you have any form of communication with anything through a freaking alarm clock? Would good ole' St. Michael send Morse code through the alarm? I was almost curious to write back and ask to see a demonstration, but who knows what can of worms I would open. To this day, I really don't know her reason for writing, as she never made any requests.

These were just samples of some of the characters involved in the paranormal. As I said, it is hard enough as it is to be taken serious when dealing with the paranormal, yet you have people like the "clock lady" that make it that much harder. I knew, without a shadow of a doubt, I did not want to be perceived as a "ghost buster" or someone who walked around, dressed in black, getting possessed by the spirits. I wanted to prove to everyone that normal people with normal lives could be successful in this hobby by taking a strictly scientific approach. By applying skeptic analysis of the work conducted, I would be seen as someone that wouldn't claim every bump in the night is a ghost. I firmly believe that in order to be successful, you must appeal to both sides: the skeptic and the believer. I knew that this approach would get me far in the eyes of others, yet there was just one problem: I couldn't really accomplish those goals if the group I was in primarily consisted of people falling over in spiritual possession. How would things change? Could it even change? No one really knew but the one thing that was for sure was that things had to change. As with anything, we would soon find out that for things to get better, they must first get a hell of a lot worse.

9

OAK ALLEY PLANTATION (VACHERIE, LA)

We were now in expansion mode and I was looking at adding members to my central chapter, which would enable us to cover a wider area. I turned to my good CPI buddy, Dustyn, to see if he wanted to join. He quickly took me up on the offer, as this is something he really enjoyed doing. A woman in Alexandria who was very interested in joining the team also contacted me. Not knowing much about the screening process, I brought her in, unaware that she had no intentions of being an asset to the group. It wasn't even a month later before I removed her from the group for simple incompetence. She then had the nerve to get mad over the fact that she never gave an ounce of participation. I never quite understood how people can want to join any type of extra-curricular group, yet not want to put any effort in it. If it is a hobby of yours, then you should be working that much harder, since it is something you supposedly love to do so much. This would prove to be one of my biggest pet peeves over the years that would follow, as I would get numerous e-mails from people wanting to join the group. After I would send them a packet with all of our guidelines, I would never hear back from them again. I guess it's like they say; good help is hard to find.

A guy contacted me one day by the name of Brandon Thomas. Brandon was about my age and lived within five miles from me. He expressed his immense interest in the paranormal and was extremely interested in joining. Steve and I set up a meeting with Brandon to meet face to face. You cannot get to know someone simply by e-mailing back and forth. I have to meet someone in person to really get a feel for him or her. Brandon's parents owned a restaurant in Pineville so we decided to meet there. I immediately clicked with Brandon, as we seemed to have many of the same interests, especially professional wrestling.

Brandon was the manager of a popular restaurant in Alexandria and had many connections with individuals in the city. Hopefully, this would help later on down the road in trying to obtain access into various establishments in the area. Another interesting thing was that the very restaurant that Brandon's parents owned was said to be active. For quite some time, there had been reports from staff and patrons alike that there were strange happenings taking place there. People reported seeing a woman in a long black dress wandering through the restaurant. In one humorous encounter, while a newly-hired employee was using the restroom, she witnessed one of the pictures on the wall literally fly across the room. The woman, who was terrified, flew out of the restroom with her pants still around her ankles. Although she had only been working there a few days, she quit on the spot.

Due to our living proximity, Brandon would now become my partner in crime, as we began visiting all of the local cemeteries with the hopes of capturing some good evidence. In the process, I was able to visit numerous cemeteries that I had never been to, including a small Baptist cemetery in Pineville. There was not much to this cemetery, except that it was an all black Baptist graveyard with some graves dating back to the early 1900's. On one particular visit there, I was taking random pictures when I noticed that I had captured one that was of interest. I was aiming at a group of graves and I noticed that on one of the headstones, there was a large ball of light on it. Initially, I thought it may have been the reflection from one of those small picture frames found on many headstones, but upon further inspection, I found there to be nothing on the stone. The light appeared to be about the size of a baseball and was orange in color. Whatever it was, it seemed to give off its own light source, as it even radiated against the stone. I then decided to walk around that particular grave and take another picture of it from a different angle. After taking the picture, I noticed that in the exact same spot that the light appeared, there was another round anomaly in the same spot, only not as visible. To this day, that is one of the more impressive orb-like objects I have captured, due to its unique luminescent characteristics.

In addition to our many cemetery visits, we would now have regular access to another location of suspected activity, which was his parents' restaurant. To make things even sweeter is that we would often go late in the night and grill up a few burgers. There's nothing like free food and ghost hunting to make for a successful evening. We visited the restaurant several times, with no strange things ever taking place. However, during one visit, we were sitting in the dining area, talking out loud to the "lady in black". We were asking for the spirit to give us some sort of a sign that they were present, whether it was in the room we were in or somewhere else. Immediately after we made the request, we heard what sounded like several dishes rattling and shuffling around. The noises sounded like they were coming from the serving area, so we walked over only to find a tall stack of small saucers. We were unsure as to what caused the saucers to rattle in that fashion but it was quite interesting to have them do so, literally on command.

Up until this point, LGH had primarily investigated private residences, besides the art museum fiasco. Things would suddenly change one day as I received a call from Brandon, who sounded extremely excited over the phone. Brandon was calling to say that the father of one of his employees was head of security at Oak Alley Plantation, in Vacherie, Louisiana. Brandon went on to say that he mentioned our group to the plantation and they were interested in having us investigate. At the time, this was beyond huge news; this was monumental.

For those of you that are unfamiliar with Oak Alley, it is one of the most well known plantations in the south. It has been featured in many major motion pictures such as: "Interview with the Vampire", "North and South", and "Primary Colors". The home received its name from the two massive rows of oak trees in front of the home. The trees are said to be over three hundred years old and planted in the 1690's, several years before the founding of New Orleans in 1718.

The home, located around a working sugar cane farm, was built between 1837 and 1839 and was constructed by George Swainy for Jacques Telesphore Roman. Jacques was the grandson of Jacques Joseph Roman, said to be the first member of the Roman family in Louisiana. Originally named *Bon Sejour* (pleasant sojourn), the home was quickly given the name "Oak Alley" by awe-inspired travelers passing along the Mississippi River. The massive home, with its twelve foot ceilings and sixteen inch walls, is adorned with twenty-eight Doric columns, expressing its French Creole and Caribbean architectural themes. Unfortunately, the home was sold in 1866 and quickly fell into despair. In 1925, the property was then purchased by Andrew and Josephine Steward, and restored to its original grandeur. After Mrs. Steward's death, the home was purchased by a preservation society and is now managed by Mr. Zeb Mayhew.

For years, there have been reports of haunted activity at Oak Alley Plantation. People have reported seeing the spirits of several young women and a male in a military uniform. Reports of people being touched, electrical devices turning on and off, and objects moving on their own have been made. No one is for certain as to who truly haunts the plantation, although many speculate Louise Roman to be involved. Louise was one of daughters of the family, who suffered a tragic accident. While fleeing from a drunken suitor, she fell down the stairs, severely cutting her leg on the iron hoop of her dress. The wound became infected, gangrene set it, and the leg had to be amputated. Louise was never the same again, soon became an introvert, and moved to St. Louis to join the Carmelite convent. Others feel that the home is haunted by the previous owner, Mrs. Josephine Stewart, as many of the visual descriptions match pictures of her when she was younger.

It literally seemed like a dream come true, as we could not believe that we would actually be getting to investigate such a historically-known location. In addition, we were going to be the first paranormal investigative group to conduct a full, scientific investigation of the plantation. We knew that this was going to be the one to make us or break us and we were not about to screw this up. We gave the good news to the rest of the group, receiving the same elated responses that we showed when we found out. Looking back, I'm surprised we weren't accused of "stealing" this case as well, but surprisingly Brandon was able to keep the credit on this one. To this day, Brandon still boasts about lining up Oak Alley; too bad he hasn't done anything since then.

The day of the investigation had finally arrived and we could not wait to make the two and a half hour drive down to Vacherie. Since the rest of the group was from southern Louisiana, the four of us in the central area decided to carpool. Dustyn and Brandon rode in one vehicle, while Steve and I in another. The plantation is located in a section of the town known as Old River Road. On this road, which stretches for miles, there are some of the most beautiful and well known plantations in the South. Taking the forty minute drive on this scenic route is truly like you are stepping back in time. As I followed the levee, I could not help but picture the way things looked in that area one hundred fifty years ago. I imagined huge steamboats along the Mississippi, pulling up to the docks to unload goods, while horse-drawn wagons came from all areas to gather whatever they needed to stock their homes. Off in the distance, I imagined the sound of large skill saws, zipping through lumber as carpenters nailed away on the rooftops of a new shed. Oh how simple, yet rewarding, things must have been back then.

As we grew nearer to the plantation, I became extremely anxious to finally see it in person. For years, I had seen pictures of those massive oak trees, forming a natural tunnel to that giant home. The time had come for me to, not only visit the home, but to be one of the first to spend the night in there to conduct a paranormal investigation. As we rounded the corner of the property, I was immediately taken back at the beauty of the grounds. Not to sound like a tree-hugging hippy, but it is amazing at how beautiful nature can be. The first thing that automatically caught my attention, were the gigantic oak trees. These trees, which were well over three hundred years old, were so old that iron supports had been imbedded into the ground, in order to brace the colossal limbs.

The rest of the group had not yet arrived so Dustyn, Steve, Brandon, and I decided to take a brief walk across the grounds. Walking through the oak trees was truly an experience as their immense size truly emitted the feeling that you were being watched. It had nothing to do with any paranormal presence or anything like that; it was simply that the trees were so large, they seemed to engulf your personal space, giving you the feeling like you were not alone. The movie buff in me soon kicked in, as I stood in certain areas of the property, reliving certain movie scenes in my head from various films. As I leaned against the very oak tree where "Lestat" feasted on the blood of a young quadroon, I was once again reminded that Louisiana has, without a doubt, some of the most intriguing history of any state.

Once everyone showed up, we made our way to introduce ourselves to the owner and the head of security. I have always been a firm believer that this is the most critical point of the night, as it is paramount that you make a good first impression on the homeowner/business owner. We were there strictly because of their kindness and generosity, so we, in turn, must show them that they made the right decision by acting in the utmost professional manner and offer the best possible services. Although I was in no leadership role at the time, I would assume that it would have only been right to have the founders of the group leading the way, as we introduced ourselves in unison. However, this was not the case, as the group leaders were trailing far behind us in an ever-so-carefree manner. As we approached the owner, we all introduced ourselves, individually thanking him for giving us the opportunity to investigate the plantation. Mr. Mayhew then asked, "Which one of you is the leader?" We all paused for a moment, as we pointed behind us in embarrassment and said, "Here they come." Moments later, one of the founders walks up with a mouth full of potato chips, looks at Mr. Mayhew, and simply says, "Hi" as she keeps walking. We all looked at each other in shock, as it was though she acted like he should have been grateful to have her there. On the contrary, it was the other way around, as we were the ones fortunate enough to have been given a chance to investigate.

Still, we knew we all had a job to do and we were not going to let someone else's lack of professionalism get in the way. In all honesty, prior to this investigation, I had really contemplated quitting the group, but I had already made some pretty good friends and I did not want to miss out on such a huge investigation. It was actually Steve that, on the way down there, talked me into staying. However, I knew my departure was only delayed a while longer as I waited for that final straw to drop. Who knew it would happen that night.

We began the investigation in the usual fashion by setting up all of our IR cameras in the home, including the third-story attic, which looked like the epitome of all creepy attics. It had these huge exposed beams that were connected with large wooden spikes, adding to the ambience of the place. As we continued to run video cable through the home, we spoke a little more with the grounds' keeper as he told us some interesting bits of information, such as the house was only sold for thirty thousand dollars in the 1800's. He then proceeded to show us an amazing picture that was taken by a tourist several years earlier. The picture was taken in one of the bedrooms on the second floor. In the room, there is a bust with a dress on it, said to have belonged to Mrs. Steward. Also in the picture, is a large wall mirror that reflects the image of the bust and dress. What makes the picture so unique is that the reflection shows the headless bust, yet in the original bust, it has a full head of hair. The picture was taken to several photograph analysts and they all returned the conclusion that the picture was original and had not been tampered with in any way.

We then began to try our luck at getting our own proof of Mrs. Stewart's presence. We broke up into several groups, spreading throughout all three floors. Brandon, Dustyn, and I took the attic area and began conducting EMF sweeps and audio recordings. The attic was completely dark and we could barely see our hands in front of our faces. Dustyn wandered off on his own on one side of the attic while Brandon and I continued to conduct EMF work. Almost immediately, we began getting considerable EMF spikes in one particular area of the attic when we would ask questions. Whatever was there seemed to interact with us, as it moved around and reacted to specific questions.

Brandon and I continued to walk around the attic, as it is one of the largest I have ever seen. We entered one little nook that had a small door in it. As Brandon opens the crawlspace door, he jokingly says, "Surprise." acting as though he caught someone hiding in the tiny room. Amazingly, when we would go over the audio, we would capture audio of what sounds just like a young girl yelling, "Oh no." The voice was very loud, as if we had caught her off guard. After listening to it numerous times, it sounded as though the girl had a real strong Cajun accent, pronouncing her words "aww non." The audio was quite clear and it was definite that it sounded like a young child, which only helped our validation of the clip, as we never allow any children on an investigation.

Minutes later, Dustyn would come scurrying back to us with a strange look on his face. When we asked him what was wrong, all he could say was, "Dude, something just freaking touched me." It was apparent that something had startled him, yet he wasn't in a panic or anything. I tried to consider all routes, asking him if he was sure he didn't brush up against any spider webs or anything like that. Dustyn assured me that the feeling was much more forceful than that caused from spider webs. He said that while we was taking random photographs, it felt as though someone literally grabbed him by his forearm. As this occurred, a strong electric surge ran through his arm, causing him to immediately drop his camera. For quite some time after, Dustyn claimed that his arm and hand remained slightly numb. The incident obviously shook Dustyn up, as he was not the same the rest of the night. Unfortunately, the experience must have been a little too personal for Dustyn, as he resigned from the group shortly after, which is why I often tell new members, "Be careful what you wish for because you just might get it."

A little later in the evening, Brandon and I would be talking in the attic, while running audio. As I said, a majority of our EVPs are captured when we are simply "shooting the bull" and not robotically asking the same boring questions over and over. In this case, Brandon and I are simply chatting when you can hear a very clear third voice say, "they killed us.' As I mentioned, there were never any documented incidents of murder on the property, yet who knows what happened that was never properly reported. Despite what you may read elsewhere, mentioning certain bedrooms are the most active areas in the home, I will be the first to disagree and say that the attic is definitely the hot spot of the house.

By this point in the night, I decided to let others have their turn in the attic while I descended to one of the monitoring stations. Luckily, other investigators began having similar experiences in the attic such as EMF spikes and strange shadows being seen in their peripheral vision. People often ask why most anomalies are only seen in the corner of your eye. The reason is that you can see much more with your peripheral vision than looking straight at a particular object. The best example of this is to look at the stars at night. If you focus at a specific star, it begins to disappear, yet you start to see all the stars around it. As soon as you focus on one of the stars that your peripheral vision was catching, it fades away as well.

As I sat at the monitoring station, I began observing something strange. I noticed that everyone had been moving around the house quite freely, except Becky and "Mr. Personality". For whatever reasons, they only stayed on the bottom floor and every time someone would come downstairs to discuss something strange that happened in the attic, I would notice their concentration would focus on them. It was as though the two were taking notes, trying to find out where all the activity for the night was coming from. I knew something wasn't right and I told Elissa to watch and see if the two wouldn't wait until the last part of the night to make their way into the attic and make their grand finale performance. Elissa jokingly said, "I give her two minutes before she falls out."

What happened next would not only be the final nail in the coffin, but would also show that Elissa may be psychic. With only about thirty minutes left in the investigation, Becky and Mr. Personality made their way to the attic, accompanied by the entire group, Mr. Zeb, and the caretaker. I swear on everything that I own, Becky did not make it but about thirty seconds into the attic before she started to stumble around as if her equilibrium was off balance. She then began saying in a panicked voice, "Black man, black man, I see a black man. Quick, somebody grab me." Just as she said that, she hit the floor like a sack of potatoes and began to convulse like an eight pound bass out of water. As her head bounced off the two hundred year old floor like a basketball, I turned to Elissa and very calmly said, "You won by a minute and thirty seconds." I then peered over towards Brandon's direction, only to see him literally put his hand on his head, shaking it in disbelief.

To make things worse, Mr. Personality pulls out a small crucifix, holds in over Becky, and begins praying over her. The owner then turns to Brandon and says, "You guys have to be joking, right?" Please keep in mind that all of these casual conversations are taking place while a woman is flopping on the floor, mocking a possession, while another individual is attempting to "exorcise the demon" from her. Never, in a million years, would I be able to describe to you the amount of shame, embarrassment, and overall disgust that we were all experiencing at that very moment. We knew right then and there that we could officially kiss our reputation and any further opportunities of getting access into any other public establishment goodbye.

Looking around the room, some were shaking their heads; others were rolling their eyes, while others simply said, "get the hell up." Brandon and I immediately rushed to Mr. Zeb to apologize for what just happened. We repeatedly tried to ensure him that what he just witnessed was not the way the rest of the group operates and we promised that something like this would never happen again. To this day, I still don't know how it happened, but Mr. Zeb and the caretaker both assured us that he completely understood where we were coming from and we did not have anything to worry about. They even expressed how they were more embarrassed for us then they were for themselves. They promised that we would still be welcomed into the plantation to investigate in the future, with the subtraction of a couple of members, of course.

Without a seconds delay, we packed all our stuff and disappeared faster than a set of rims at a rap concert. We figured maybe if we would leave fast enough, we could catch up with our pride that was way ahead of us. Nothing was verbally mentioned regarding the future of the group and everyone's status, yet we all subconsciously knew that things needed to change drastically and something big was about to happen. We just didn't know when or how, yet I was pretty sure that I was going to be the catalyst to get the ball rolling.

Luckily, to lighten up an extremely tense night, Steve had a little "accident" on the way home that night. Steve is a verified narcoleptic, literally falling fast asleep within seconds. This made for a long road trip, as Steve was sound asleep in the first ten minutes, while I had to make the long drive home. About an hour into the drive, I told Steve that we had to stop for something to drink, before I fell asleep at the wheel. After making a quick pit stop, Steve made the mistake of getting a large cup of coffee. We got back in the car and headed home. We weren't down the highway but fifteen minutes before Steve fell back asleep. The next thing I heard was, "OWWW. Stop the car." I slammed on the breaks and came to a stop as Steve flew out of the car, drenched in hot coffee. What was even funnier was that it was about thirty degrees that night, so when he bolted from the car, the cold air caused the coffee to steam off his crotch. There was poor Steve and his "blazing crotch", doing this little jig that looked like an epileptic cripple on the side of the road.

It must have been something in the air that night, because it seemed as if everyone was convulsing that night. Looking back on the whole ordeal, I cannot help but laugh. I can still not fathom how someone can try and pull stuff like that. To this day, I am uncertain as to if the actions that night were for attention, an attempt to sabotage the group, or, in the rare case, an actual spiritual possession. I had already had a hard time believing in the validity of those who claimed to be "sensitive". However, after that night, my beliefs were definitely in the crapper. Don't get me wrong, there are some very legitimate individuals out there with gifted sensitive abilities, but they are few and far between. I would say that about 80 percent of those who claim to have abilities are as fake as a three dollar bill. I often like to use the analogy of someone who knows karate: those who really know karate are the ones who never talk about it. The ones who brag all the time are the ones who don't know the difference between a wristlock and a wristwatch.

Despite our second fiasco, we still could say we investigated Oak Alley Plantation. It would be several months until the gracious owners would allow us to return for a follow up. Only this time, we would be exorcist-free and better than ever. I cannot thank the owners and staff of Oak Alley for really putting us on the map with that first investigation and for having the patience to give us a second chance.

As I said, I knew something big was going to have to change. The question was: Where do we go from here? For the answer, I simply went back to my old CPI stomping grounds to possibly relive the idea of running my own group. Maybe this time, we could spread that "sin" a little further than CenLa.

10

THE BIRTH OF LOUISIANA SPIRITS

After the Oak Alley "Flop Fest", it was safe to say that everyone in the group was fed up with the way it was being operated. The week after the investigation, we all began talking about leaving the group. The only problem was that we still immensely enjoyed investigating and did not want to give that up just yet. I knew I had the drive to dedicate the time required to run a group, but would I have the members? I began to suggest the idea to several of the group members, which they were all pretty receptive to. I wouldn't quite say that it was a mutiny, as I was simply trying to test the waters to see if others were equally interested in forming a new group.

    As I mentioned earlier, I wanted to be in a group that relied solely on a scientific approach and skeptical analysis of collected evidence. I didn't want to be known as the group whose main tool was a sensitive. I would much rather have a simple interesting audio clip that I could present to the public, as opposed to two or three people saying, "I felt a strange presence in that room." Sure, that approach may be sufficient in the immediate paranormal community, as most individuals in the field could buy that as a method of investigating. However, paranormal enthusiasts are not the only people we deal with. Sooner or later, every investigative team is going to deal with either a non-believer, or worse, a member of the media. When they do, a simple accusation from an individual claiming they felt a spirit in a home is not going to cut it when dealing with the masses. Otherwise, you will end up with another art museum fiasco, as with the one we had.

Despite the fact that we were all unhappy and wanted to quit, the nice guy in me thought that maybe we could give the group leaders another chance. I thought that maybe if we could all have a huge "pow-wow", where we could all express our concerns, the founders would see that things needed to change and would take the appropriate actions to make things better. I proceeded to arrange an emergency chat meeting for the following night, where we could all get everything out on the table, without fear of reprimand. Still, knowing the personalities of the founders, I knew that the meeting would not go well, due to the simple fact that we would be questioning their leadership abilities. We knew that topic was the quickest way to piss them off, as we had all witnessed the two argue many times over the exact same thing.

The night of the meeting arrived, as I prepared for the worst. I made sure to clean out my LGH mailbox account, knowing that a potential hissy fit could occur at any given time and I could lose all my mail messages, as we all had numerous times during many of the founders' spats. I had even begun to toy with several group names, just in case things got so bad, we had to jump ship. If my memory serves me correct, I think I even started working on a new logo for the potential group, which consisted of a simple image of an alligator standing next to a gravestone. Still, I was just letting my imagination get carried away, as I figured I would have no need for any new group name or logo since everything was going to probably be resolved. Lucky for me, I didn't delete the logo.

Just about everyone from the group attended the meeting, which was about twelve people. I think one of the founders must have known that something was up, as she immediately said, "ok, what's all this about?" I figured it didn't pay to beat around the bush, so I quickly went into my reason for setting up the meeting. I began by politely bringing up Becky's antics at Oak Alley and everyone was in fear that our reputation would soon be ruined, if it hadn't already. Without a seconds delay, Becky quickly retaliated with her defense. She went into this huge spill about how she has had legitimate abilities since she was a child and people like "us" have always tormented her and made fun of her skills. Mr. Personality then made the mistake of including his timid little self in the conversation, defending Becky. This was all the fuel I needed, as I already couldn't stand him. I then proceeded to unleash my opinion of him, which consisted of some pretty choice words. Luckily, others in the group were also fed up with his crucifix-wielding, Father Merrick-like antics, as they also joined the rebuttal in my defense. Feeling outnumbered and defeated, Mr. Personality made a last ditch effort at a comeback by simply saying he hated me and he wanted to kill me. Can you believe it; death threats in ghost hunting.

This did not sit lightly with the founders, as they were very good friends with Becky and Mr. Personality. I then set my sights on the group leaders, telling them how the entire group was quite disgruntled at the way things were being ran. We were tired of being drug into the middle of their little spats, which seemed to become more and more frequent. Before I could get another word out of my mouth, one of the founders began to unleash an onslaught of insults that seemed to come completely out of thin air. In a fashion only suitable for power-hungry individuals with no leadership abilities, she went with the traditional response by saying, "you know what, if you don't like the way things are ran, you can get the hell out."

It was at this monumental cornerstone that I immediately made my final decision. I became so outraged I could barely even type what I had to say. Mustering up my last bits of composure, I put the nail in the coffin, by saying that not only was I quitting LGH, but the rest of the group was following too, and we would now be starting our own group. Needless to say, this was officially when the "fecal matter struck the oscillating device", as the founder literally blew a gasket. She proceeded to say that this was a conspiracy and that we had all plotted against her and her group. After trying to bring everyone to her level by saying we would never be able to run our own group, she then decided to take the dirty route, attempting to turn us on one another. She tried to start the "he said-she said" game, yet no one was falling for it, as we all knew she was very capable of putting the "d" in drama.

It was now apparent that everyone had seen the tactics the group leaders were willing to take to remain in control. No one wanted to be around faux colleagues that were willing to stab them in the back at the drop of a dime. In a last ditch effort, one of them even tried to play the sympathy card, claiming that the group was her life and, without it, there was no need to live anymore. By this point I did not have a compassionate bone in my body, encouraging her that was the best idea she had so far.

In the weeks that would follow the "chat meeting from hell", which it later became known as, things would get very stressful for me, as I began receiving threatening e-mails from the former group leader. In an extremely pathetic attempt to get revenge, they began threatening that they would start rumors of infidelity, simply to cause distinction in my home life, which is about one of the lowest things one can do. Fortunately, the Coonass in me does not take well to threats, often causing me to challenge them to the limits. I now knew that the only way to really seek my own form of revenge was not to stoop to their level, but to basically "kill them with kindness", a motto I have lived by most of my life. I knew that if I could simply start up my own group and successfully run it using my scientific approach, it would piss them off much more than if I would've gone blow for blow with them.

 I now officially had my own paranormal investigative group. The first matter at hand was, of course, what to name it. Although I wasn't quite sure on a name, I knew I did not want to go with the traditional acronym, seen pretty much with all groups. With what seemed like a million and one groups in existence, everyone was naming themselves with a title that could be broken down into some sort of acronym. People began to get so carried away with it, they weren't even realizing what the acronyms were saying. They were trying so hard to find titles that could spell a single word, they were making asses out of themselves. In one of the best examples; I was surfing the web as I always do, and came across one group, whose name would stick in my mind forever. They called themselves the Central Organization that Research Unknown Paranormal Things, or CORUPT, for short. I am curious to see how many cases they get with a name like that. I can literally hear their motto: "CORUPT: A name you can trust." A while back at a paranormal conference, I met a group whose name abbreviated into SPIT. For some unknown reason, their founder got upset with me when I asked if they had a sister group called SWALLOW. I know, I can be such a jerk.

 In an attempt to make a mockery of the whole acronym dilemma, I once created a faux group called Spirit Hunters Investigative Team, better known as SHIT. Again, I have no life, so I even took it as far as creating their own Website, which portrayed the created characters as complete hillbillies, using some of the most primitive tools, such as fishing nets, to conduct their SHIT investigations. Their site became pretty elaborate, actually being more extensive than many legit sites out there. All of their investigations consisted of old decrepit homes, except a "haunted river" called SHIT creek. My favorite was their demonologist, Father Jimmy, better known to the group as holy SHIT. The group became quite a hit with the paranormal community, as it poked fun at how there are actual groups out there that really have no clue what they are doing, only making fools of themselves. Although their Website is no longer in operation, I will never forget their motto: "Spirit Hunters Investigative Team: You got ghosts, we'll wipe em clean."

Knowing I wanted to stay away from crazy acronym-style names, I began to think of a name that would be specific to our region. My initial ideas were "Ghosts Along the Bayou" and "Spirits of the South". Looking back, I find those names to be pretty corny and am glad I never chose them. After much deliberation, I thought that it would be best to keep it simple. Taking into account that we are from Louisiana and we search for proof of spirits, why not put the two together, calling ourselves "Louisiana Spirits". It seemed to have simplicity, yet was interesting enough to leave people wandering as to who and what was this group. We then took the simplicity further, often abbreviating the name into "LaSpirits".

The next step was that we needed to have a Website. I have always been an artist at heart, nearly picking art as my college major. I am a firm believer in making eye catching advertisements to draw peoples' attention to a product, or in this case, a Website. With LGH, the site was extremely bland and literally one-dimensional. Being I graduated with a degree in Computer Information Technology; I literally eat, breathe, and sleep computers. Two of my favorite areas are Website designing and graphic arts. I knew that I wanted to make an eye-catching site that was a little different than most of the traditional, template-based sites, that I seemed to see all the time. The approach I wanted to take was a dark looking site, yet still looked professional, not looking like a Halloween site. With this concept, I would like to think I created the style I like to call "Executive Goth".

One of my more dominant traits is that I do not like to do anything half-ass. I have always been an "all or nothing" type of person. I refused to slap up a temporary "under construction" site with broken links and such, just to say we had a site. My first night that I activated the site, I stayed up all night, having to go to work in the morning. I was absolutely exhausted, yet we had a fully functional Website the very first night. From that starting point, I continued adding as much information as I thought people would like to see on a paranormal Website. I would like to think that we have one of the more informative paranormal Websites out there, as it covers just about every facet of the field. After biting my lip for ten chapters, I finally have a spot where I can plug our web address, so please check us out at www.laspirits.com.

Now that we had a mission statement and a Website, all that was left was coverage area and structure. Luckily, we didn't have to build from the ground up, as with most new groups. We already had a group of twelve people from across the state, which had all jumped ship together, so we already had the structure to build off of. I decided that the only way we could grow would be to cover the entire state and not limit ourselves to a certain city or region. I divided the group into four chapters: central, northern, southeast, and southwest. Each chapter would have their own case manager that would organize the cases for that particular area, serving as a much more organized structure. To this day, this method works extremely well as it not only allows each chapter to feel that they are in charge of their own area, but also ensures that no particular group, including myself, gets overloaded with cases.

We then looked at updating the methods of obtaining an investigation. As any investigation teams can agree, this is the hardest part of being in a group. It can often be very awkward to speak with a homeowner or business owner, trying to be allowed to investigate their location. This is especially hard if the potential client is not very receptive to having an investigation conducted. This normally is the case with business owners of known haunted locations. An even larger obstacle to overcome is if the business owner has had a bad experience with other, less experienced, groups. In many cases, you are literally "selling your group" to that individual, coercing them to see that you are a professional group that follow strict rules and guidelines. This is why it is essential that the member attempting to obtain the investigation has good people skills and won't take no for an answer. I often tell my members, "The squeaky wheel gets the grease," meaning that the more persistent you are, in most cases, you are able to succeed. However, one must have a level of common sense to know when they are being persistent versus being simply psychotic. I figured that the easiest way to request an investigation was to simply submit a lengthy investigation request letter. The letter would literally serve as a resume, telling the potential client who we are, where we have been, and how we conduct our investigations. I would say that in at least 70 percent of our attempts, the request letter has been all that was needed to get the investigation.

Once the investigation was obtained, we then had to consider other forms of paperwork. Another important part of an investigation is the preliminary. The preliminary consist of simply meeting with the client, getting a feel for them and to basically visit the location during daylight hours. Anyone who has done this before can agree; any location looks totally different in total darkness. In addition, if the location is in poor condition, this is also a good time to annotate any structural dangers, such as holes in the floor or any other potential hazards. During the preliminary, I felt that it would be a good time to sit down with the client and ask any questions such as the history of the location and whether or not they have had any strange experiences. To simplify this process, we created a questionnaire form, which covered many areas, which could allow us to get a better look at the situation. In some cases, the questionnaire can assist us in determining that an investigation is not even required. We have sometimes determined that what the homeowner has initially deemed as paranormal has been negated due to the fact that they have recently been on specific types of medications, causing them various side effects such as dizziness, paranoia, and hallucinations.

Another very important issue when dealing with being on other peoples' property is liability. We did not want the client to be concerned about what would happen if one of our members injured themselves during an investigation or if the personal property of the client or investigator was damaged. To resolve this, we created a liability waiver form, which waived any liability from the client, should one of us be injured in any way while on their property. In addition, the form also made our members liable if we were to accidentally damage any of the client's property during our stay. In many cases, the simple fact that we offer this waiver greatly reassures the client, as they initially see that we are serious enough to offer this type of protection. Fortunately, to this date, we have never had to worry about liability being an issue, as our investigators have always acted in the most professional of manners.

I then looked at ways to get our name out in the general and paranormal communities. I began exchanging web links with as many different paranormal Websites as I could think of, with the hopes that we could begin to get established. Several of us even had business cards made; dropping them off at coffee shops and the information desks of reportedly haunted public venues. As I mentioned, I have often been accused of being a "media whore" and that I am only doing this for fame and fortune. All I can say is that if those are my only aspirations, than I have done a horrible job, because I can say with a straight face, I have not accomplished either one.

Let's face it; everyone wants access into high-profile haunted locations. In order to do so, you must acquire some sort of resume, listing all the previous places you have been. In many cases, when I try to obtain access into a popular establishment, I am often asked if we have any references, so the client can verify the quality of our work. Without any references, I highly doubt we would have ever been able to investigate many of the locations we have been to. This is why I am a firm believer in getting our name out there to the local community. By being in local newspapers, television, and magazines, we allow the general public to see how we operate and luckily, because of our skeptical approach, we have always received considerably good reviews. As I learned from the museum, the media can make a mountain out of a mole hill. The key is to not even give them a speck of dirt to form that mole hill to elaborate on. Taking the approach of "I am not saying this place is haunted and if I determine that it isn't, I don't mind saying it", makes you ten times more credible than the group that feels that they are obligated to prove that a place is active. Groups that have that pressure of "producing" are far more likely to generate poor evidence and, in many cases, make a fool of themselves, especially with the hard core skeptics.

I hate to jinx myself, but I can honestly say that we have always had an extremely good relationship with any media organization that we have worked with. As I have said, our approach has allowed us to be portrayed as individuals that do believe in the paranormal, yet are not close-minded enough to not admit that a majority of the strange occurrences reported have logical explanations. It also helps that, for the most part, we are all fairly normal people. As with anything, your image reflects a great deal of whom you are and how you carry yourself. If the public sees a group consisting of long-haired freaks, dressed in black, and flopping on the ground, then it is safe to say that they will not take you very seriously.

Approaching every investigation from a skeptical point of view has been my forte from day one. It is always more rewarding to approach each investigation with the notion that the place does not contain paranormal activity. With this approach, any evidence collected is a bonus, plus it does not discourage you as bad when you are able to debunk an event. I will be the first to admit, it gets extremely frustrating when you constantly debunk events. Even though your approach is skeptical, you can't help but want to find legitimate evidence. When you find something that initially seems strange, whether it be on video, audio, or photographic, to be able to debunk it is often bitter-sweet. Part of you is discouraged that the evidence you captured was not paranormal, while part of you has a feeling of accomplishment, knowing that you are not short-changing yourself, your group, and the client.

A prime example of this was when we conducted our initial investigation of Brandon's parent's restaurant. We had set up our IR cameras, which were run throughout the restaurant. One of the areas said to be a "hot spot" was the dry food storage area, where shadows were often seen and objects were thrown from the shelves. I placed one of the cameras on the rear shelf, giving a good range of coverage. Later in the night, several investigators, armed with a handheld video camera, would station themselves in this room to obtain audio and video recordings. Days after the investigation, one of the group members sent me a segment of video from her handheld. She was extremely excited, stating that she thought she had captured video of a shadowed figure, walking across the kitchen area. When I watched the video, I was initially astonished, as I could plainly see what looked like the silhouette of a person walk from one side of the kitchen to the other. After showing it to the rest of the group, they were equally impressed by the footage, all thinking we had captured an actual apparition on camera. However, the skeptic in me felt that this video was too good to be true. I remembered that I also had an IR camera in the storage area, which was pointed in the same direction as the handheld. I hoped that maybe the IR camera also captured this shadow, so I could have something else to compare the original video to. After matching up the times on both cameras, I was able to find when the anomaly took place on the IR camera. What the handheld video did not show was that behind it, there was an investigator conducting EMF sweeps. The IR camera, which was behind the investigator showed that as her hand was sweeping from left to right, a shadow casts of her hand that was holding the EMF meter onto the wall. The position of her hand and the meter strongly resembled an upper torso and head. With the naked eye, the shadow could not be visible, as the investigators were in total darkness. However, the shadow being created was from an IR camera, which was only visible by the IR capabilities of the handheld. How's that for extensive debunking abilities. Needless to say, the entire group, including myself, was very disappointed that we had found the culprit to our shadow, yet I felt that we had to follow this type of approach in order for us to remain true to ourselves.

Unfortunately, this would not be the same approach taken by many other groups out there. I can't help but laugh when I see Websites out there, showing off "evidence" said to be paranormal, yet it is obvious it is something quite explainable. I am unsure as to this is due to pure stupidity, ignorance, or lack of conscience. What's even more frustrating is that when you try and educate these types of people, they immediately get defensive, refusing to hear any other explanations than the ones that they have. A good example is of a Website that I came across that had a picture of a supposed "spirit orb". The picture was taken in the middle of the day and was of a large headstone in a cemetery. Next to the headstone was a huge ball of light, said to be the anomaly. Within seconds of viewing the picture, it was obvious that this alleged "spirit orb" was simply the sun barely peaking around the headstone. Even though the amount of the sun that was visible was small, it caused a huge glare that gave the effect of a large ball of light. This was further apparent by the shadows from the trees, which were coming from the direction of the light. It amazes me how people can do such stupid things and have the nerve to stand behind them so diligently. Then again, these are probably the same individuals that were fooled into paying money for homemade "certifications" in paranormal investigating. As with any scam, I can only assume that by purchasing a phony certification, you are taught how to conduct phony evidence analysis. Again, you get what you pay for.

With our group infrastructure laid out, we were a pretty well running organization. Although in our youth, we began getting several investigations of private residences and an occasional business. We began to be featured on several paranormal-based radio programs, allowing us to get our name out to fellow enthusiasts. Our biggest project during our early beginning was when I was contacted by Bill Murphy, a California film maker. It must have been fate, because our Website had not even been up a month when I received Bill's e-mail. Bill was originally from New Orleans and always had an immense love for the mystery of the south. At the time, he was interested in filming a documentary on the possibilities that there was an increase in paranormal activity in New Orleans after Hurricane Katrina. Although the idea was a good one, I told Bill that New Orleans was still literally a war zone and, even if there was an increase in activity, there would be no one there to even validate new events with past experiences. Fortunately, Bill decided to broaden his subject matter and decide to follow us on several locations throughout Louisiana. Bill then asked me to choose three locations that would make for good segments in the film. Without a seconds delay, I immediately said that we wanted to return to Ft. Derussy, the Jones's residence, and Oak Alley Plantation.

The entire experience was extremely enjoyable, as we had never done anything like that before. What was even more fortunate was that we actually obtained legitimate evidence at all three locations to add to the intrigue of the documentary. As I mentioned earlier, the crew experienced mass battery drain at Ft. Derussy, legitimate EVPs and EMF spikes at Oak Alley, and moving doors at the Jones's residence. The result of our little group endeavor was a documentary titled "World's Largest Ghost Town: A Post-Katrina Investigation." The documentary further enabled us to get our name out there to the masses, adding another accomplishment to our growing resume. I would like to greatly appreciate Bill and his crew for such an enjoyable experience, as I will always be in debt to him for taking the time to give such a new group the opportunity to spotlight our abilities.

Our group was now up and running and an excellent pace. We were getting our name out to the public, obtaining quality investigations, and now were featured in an actual documentary. All this took place in our first six months of existence. Not too bad for a group that had originated from floor-floppin' fiascos. Despite our quick growth, I knew that we would have to keep up the pace if we were going to continue to be successful. Seeing all the poorly-operated groups out there, I was interested in now doing some type of educating to individuals interested in becoming an investigator. No fees, no cheesy certificates, just simple workshops or seminars, that would allow us to get our name out there, while educating the public. Now, all we had to do, was to find a venue large enough to accommodate a large group of people and, oh yeah, it had to be haunted too.

11
THE SHREVEPORT MUNICIPAL AUDITORIUM (SHREVEPORT, LA)

With the group up and running to a quick success, I relied heavily on the group structure we had implemented. I looked to the assistance of my co-founders and case managers to make sure that everything was going smoothly. Due to their patience with the group and their leadership capabilities, I had decided to make Brandon and Todd my co-founders, as they had proved to be capable of assisting in running the group. Todd was also the case manager for the northern chapter, as his primary duty was to obtain and organize investigations for his chapter. Todd and his chapter were off to a great start, landing numerous investigations and were covered by several media organizations. Todd would eventually get married and move to Texas, causing us to lose a huge asset to the group. I can only imagine how much more we would have accomplished if Todd would have stayed in the group. Luckily, Todd did not lose his love for the paranormal, as he started his own group when he moved. Serving as a sister group to Louisiana Spirits, Texas Spirits was born. Before Todd's departure from the group, he would probably be best known for bringing us an investigation that would truly allow us to be commonly known in the northern portion of the state. This investigation would be of the Shreveport Municipal Auditorium.

The Shreveport Municipal Auditorium was built in 1929 in a section of downtown Shreveport, Louisiana, known as Ledbetter Heights, named after famed musician Huddie "Leadbelly" Ledbetter. The massive five-story building contains a three-level tier system, capable of seating nearly four thousand people. For several recitals, attendance levels were said to hit a record of over five thousand. The exterior is extremely ornate, containing intricate brick work and carved limestone. The interior is said to be perfectly built in regards to acoustics, allowing sound to literally conform to the building, making it the ideal location for music events. In its many years of operation, the auditorium has been home to literally every type of public event, such as orchestras, concerts, political speeches, group meetings, and my personal favorite, professional wrestling.

The auditorium would be best known for its radio program named, "The Louisiana Hayride", which first aired on April 3, 1948. The Louisiana Hayride, which was a weekly showcase of up and coming performers, soon became a huge success in the south, being surpassed only by the famous Grand Ole Opry. Due to the high quality of new performers, the auditorium received the nickname "the Cradle to the Stars," due to the fact that so many nationally-renown musicians began their careers at the venue. Famed performers such as Hank Williams Sr., Johnny Cash, and Slim Whitman all began their illustrious careers here, yet none would be as huge as the first performance of a Mississippi native on October 16,

1954. A little-known performer by the name of Elvis Presley made his on-stage debut here and quickly grew into a huge success. Performing for only eighteen dollars per show, Elvis would eventually be discovered by Colonel Tom Parker, where his contract would be purchased for ten thousand dollars.

As an added bit of interesting information, as stars such as "The King" were shake, rattling, and rolling across the stage, a very different story was being told under their very feet. As some of the biggest names in country music were performing for the public, the portion of the basement immediately under the stage was serving as the city morgue. It sounds morbid to think about it but it's kind of humorous to know that while ole Hank Williams was "moaning a honky tonk song", corpses were be being prepared for the embalming table. However, the location of the morgue could have been extremely convenient, in case a poorly-performing musician happened to "die" on stage.

For years, there had been vague rumors of several strange occurrences taking place at the auditorium, but no one had ever conducted a formal investigation of the massive building. Todd and his chapter would soon change this as they would diligently work with the staff of the auditorium, in allowing us to investigate. Fortunately, everything would work out as planned, as we were given permission to conduct the first ever paranormal investigation of this historic location.

I was unable to attend the investigation that night. I deeply regret missing it, as the night seemed to be interesting, to say the least. Todd and his group arrived at the auditorium and began to set up all of the surveillance equipment. Despite the fact that we were well-equipped for most investigations, our coverage area was quickly dwarfed due to the size of the enormous building. This handicap forced the group to focus primarily on the areas of suspected activity, such as the former morgue area, the stage, and the dressing rooms. One particular dressing room was called the "Elvis Presley dressing room" as it once was used by, you guessed it. The room is adorned with various pieces of Elvis memorabilia and is still in the original condition that it was in when it was regularly used by the famed musician.

The investigation began with the group spreading throughout the stage, basement, and dressing rooms. One of the investigators stood alone on the dark stage, while another sat in the seating area with a voice recorder. The investigator on the stage then began to ask questions out loud such as "What is your name?" and "Are you attached to this place?" Several minutes later, the investigators heard what sounded like several claps from the balcony area. The investigator asked to whoever was present, if they could clap again. Almost instantly, the two heard another round of clapping, which was fortunately caught on the recorder. The astonished pair then made their way to the area where the clapping seemed to originate from, only to find that no one was present.

As interesting as this personal experience was, it would not compare to the popularity of the recorded evidence captured in the Elvis Presley dressing room. A male and female investigator was quietly sitting in the dressing room, taking audio recordings. As I had mentioned, electronic voice phenomena are one of the more intriguing types of evidence out there, simply due to the fact that you do not hear anything until you replay the audio recorded. It is at this time, there is the potential that you can hear a voice that was not there before. People often ask if it is possible to hear an EVP with your naked ears as it is being recorded. Being the term is an electronic voice phenomenon, which means that you can only hear the voice through electronic means. If you are able to hear a sound or voice without the use of a recording device, then you are simply experiencing voice phenomena.

What was captured that evening would truly go down as one of the most interesting, yet controversial, EVPs we would ever capture. As the male and female are having a conversation, you can hear a third voice clearly say, "I love Johnny Cash." I will be the first to admit that when I initially heard the recording I thought it was too good to be true, figuring that someone was playing a joke on me. However, Todd was being extremely adamant on the validity of the recording and, knowing how serious Todd is when investigating, I knew that he was legitimately sincere when he said that the recording was authentic. Now that I was sold, there came the daunting task of putting this amazing piece of evidence out for the public to scrutinize. I knew that when the public would hear it, they would also immediately say that it was too good to be true.

Fortunately, Todd and his group would be accompanied that night by a member of one of the major newspapers in Shreveport. This would result in a very good article that would make the front page several days later. The highlight of the article was, of course, the interesting audio clip that we had obtained. The article was a huge success, giving us nearly a thousand hits on the Website in the first day. However, despite all those who were equally impressed with our findings, there were those, as I expected, who immediately began to make the allegations that we faked the evidence for attention. This has always been a problem in the paranormal community. Hard core skeptics around the boards will constantly slam and bash every questionable piece of evidence presented, claiming that they need to see something more impressive and concrete. However, when you do present something of more interest, those skeptics automatically say it is too good to be true and that the evidence was faked. It has, and always will be, a never-ending battle with these types of people. The most sensible thing to do is to politely brush these individuals off, as you will never be able to satisfy them. Constantly bickering with these people will prove to be useless, as they will ultimately have their mind set on the outcome, the same as when dealing with the hardcore believers. Nothing you say or do will ever change their minds, so it is best to simply leave them walking in circles in their own ignorant, close-minded world.

Now that we had officially placed the Shreveport Municipal Auditorium on the paranormal map, people began to quickly flock to the location to try their luck at their own investigation. The day that Todd made a return trip to present an evidence release to the staff, there was another group present from another state, preparing to conduct an investigation while filming a small documentary. Small local groups then began adding the auditorium to their sites, advertising it as a haunted location in Louisiana. Constant interest by local ghost hunting enthusiasts would ultimately cause the staff of the auditorium to offer "haunted nighttime tours" of the building to limited guests, allowing them to basically wander around the building, which was dimly lit to add to the ambience. This was all so new to the area, as no one had ever openly depicted the auditorium as containing activity, until we did. To this day, we would like to think that we have contributed an increased level of tourism to such a history-enriched portion of Shreveport.

With such an intense paranormal interest now enveloping the auditorium, I knew that we had to do something big to allow the public access to conduct their own form of investigating, while learning about, what we thought to be, the proper methods of investigating. After some intense brainstorming with Todd and Brandon, we decided to offer a paranormal seminar at the auditorium. The seminar would consist of a one hour presentation on the basics of paranormal investigating such as the types of hauntings, evidence, and equipment, and how to take a scientific and skeptical approach to investigating. We would then divide the group into smaller groups and chaperone them throughout the various sections of the building, allowing them to conduct their own investigations. We presented the idea to the staff of the auditorium to see what they thought, hopefully approving the event. Fortunately, they loved the idea and gave us the green light.

Although the venue could hold many more people, we decided to limit the attendance to seventy people. Having more people, would take away from the "creep factor" of the actual investigation. I would then create a digital presentation, covering pretty much everything you previously read in the "Ghost Hunting 101" chapter of this book. To add a little self-promotion in the event, we decided to have an information table at the door, where we handed out brochures, business cards, and complimentary "LaSpirits" ink pens. We then decided to take it one step further, and raffle off a "ghost hunting kit", containing numerous items such as an EMF meter, voice recorder, IR thermometer, and 35 mm camera. This would prove to be a huge success, as a guest could come out with a very nice equipment bundle for only a few bucks. These raffles would be used in many of our future speaking engagements and become very popular.

To our surprise, the event would sell out in only a few weeks. We were extremely excited to offer this event to the public, as it would pave the way for many other events. The event, which was the first of its kind in Shreveport, made news on every media plateau. Todd and I were featured on several morning radio and television shows, promoting the event, while allowing the public to get a look at the operations of our group. One of the many things I can proudly say that ghost hunting has allowed me to do is to overcome by fear of speaking in front of groups. I can remember in high school and college, I was absolutely mortified to speak in front of more than two people. As we began giving more speeches regarding the paranormal, I became more and more confident. Now I am able to speak in front of several hundred people and not think twice about it. The same applies to radio and television appearances. As with anything, repetition can allow you to get accustomed to pretty much anything. It also doesn't hurt when you are speaking about a topic that you are actually interested in.

The actual seminar went off without a hitch and was a huge success. Everyone enjoyed the presentation, proving to be quite useful for those in attendants, as they all seemed to take our advice and use some of the investigating techniques that we had recommended. If I recall correctly, no one had any substantial paranormal activity take place, yet they all had a great time roaming around in the dark, getting a shot at being an investigator for the night. On a personal note, while sitting alone in the upper tier, I heard what sounded like someone dropped several coins immediately behind me. I got up and searched for quite some time, but could not find anything that could have made that noise. Unfortunately, there had been a rock concert there the night before, and all I found during my search were several piles of old vomit and a used tampon. Oh, the joys of the hunt.

Earlier that evening, I was told to visit Oakland Cemetery, which is located directly across the street to the auditorium. According to reports, the cemetery is the oldest in Shreveport, opening in 1845, and houses some of the most influential individuals in the city's history. I was taken through the cemetery that afternoon by the director of the auditorium. Tourists be warned, as the cemetery is not in the best section of town and it's highly recommended to visit only during daylight hours.

As I entered the cemetery, I was immediately taken back by the ornate design of many of these tombstones, especially the tall, obelisk-style monuments. Most people do not realize how much symbolism is represented on the numerous headstones in a cemetery. In many cases, you can often tell what type of person the deceased individual was simply by looking at their headstone. For example, a rose with a broken stem or a lamb represents a deceased child. An image of an open book represents an individual that has died at a young age, while a closed book could relate to an individual who has live a long, active life. Something as simple as a few letters can often represent a much more elaborate meaning. For example, most everyone has seen the simple letters "XP" on a headstone or on various religious items. This normally stands for an individual who was a devoted Christian. The letters "XP" represent the Greek letters "*Chi*" and "*Rho*", meaning "*Christos*", the Latin word for Christ. In legend, these letters were also said to be the symbol on the shield of Constantine when he battled Maxentius during his crusade for Christianity.

Walking around the cemetery, I immediately noticed how cluttered all the graves were, except in one particular area, which seemed to be completely empty. When I questioned the director as to why this area was empty, I was quickly reminded that looks can be deceiving. I was told that this apparently desolate area was actually a mass burial plot for victims of a yellow fever epidemic and was known as the "cotton patch". Rumors are that the plot contains hundreds of individuals, literally piled on top one another, serving as a crude reminder of the horrors caused due to deadly epidemics such as yellow fever.

As I neared the end of my tour, I was reminded that there was one more grave that I had to see. The grave belonged to a Miss Cora Lee Wilson and was said to be the most interesting grave there. Miss Cora was said to be a wealthy socialite in the 1880's, during the booming era of Shreveport. I was expecting to see a large, ornate plot, decorated with multiple designs. As I approached her burial site, I was surprised to see a decrepit grave, literally falling to pieces. When I walked around to the other side, I was shocked to see that the grave was in such disrepair, the entire front panel of bricks had completely fallen over, exposing a small wrought iron casket. The casket looked as if it was intended for a five year old, due to its size. However, I was quickly advised that Miss Cora was actually an adult when she passed, yet she was extremely small in stature. Still, I couldn't help but remember reading in the past, where the limbs of individuals were often broke or cut off, in order to fit the person in their pre-made casket. Unless Miss Cora was a midget, I still do not see how she could have fit in the casket, which measured about four feet long and only about ten inches across. I asked the director of the auditorium if there had ever been an attempt to seal up the grave. She advised me that the front wall had been re-bricked numerous times, yet that one particular side always seemed to eventually fall back apart. For a good look at the grave of Miss Cora Lee Wilson, you need look no further that the cover of this book.

As I mentioned, the initial seminar proved to be a huge success, paving the way for numerous other speaking engagements. We would hold another seminar in the auditorium about a year later, with equal success. Keep in mind though, it can get quite challenging, corralling seventy or so people throughout a five story building in the dark. I can remember during our first event there, I was assigned to chaperoning ten people throughout various areas at specific times. At the time, we were assigned to investigate the dressing rooms, which were located on the first two floors. The third floor consisted of several maintenance rooms. I had specifically told my group to stay only on the first two floors, as it would be easier to keep track of them. I thought that we had prepared for everything prior to the event, being that I am a very thorough person. However, I did not stop to think that by having some type of event on a Friday night in Shreveport, some of the attendees may arrive a little "under the influence". Of course, with my luck, I ended up with the group that must have come straight from a twelve-step program, as over half of them smelled like a brewery. For the most part, they were all listening pretty well, until towards the end of the night, I could not account for two of the members. After searching the first two floors to no avail, I made my way to the third floor to search the maintenance rooms. There, in one of the mechanical rooms, I found the inebriated couple, making out. I felt like a damn chaperone at a high school dance, as I flashed the light on them and they came scurrying out like two little tipsy ants.

One of the most entertaining things about holding these events is that you always meet quite an eclectic group of people, all with quite an array of personalities. You try your best to remain professional and treat everyone with respect, as they all have the same interest as you do, but sometimes it takes everything in you not to erupt into laughter when you deal with some of these people. Let's face it, not everyone who has a love for the paranormal are the most level headed of people. I am sure I will be bashed over this comment, but some are basically just loony. A part of me wants to feel sorry for them, yet sometimes I just can't help but laugh.

One of the most classic examples was during one of our public events, where we allowed the general public to partake in an investigation. We had instructed everyone prior to the event to bring any and all equipment that they had, such as cameras, flashlights, and voice recorders. One particular individual, whom we quickly labeled the "Flava Flav of Ghost Hunting", would remain etched in my mind for eternity. The woman seemed to be in her late forties or early fifties. Apparently, she either tremendously misunderstood my speech or she slept through it, because she seemed a little confused on what equipment was actually considered as useful. Imagine an older woman, wearing combat boots, with a large eight-inch, wall-mounted thermometer tied around her neck. Yes, you heard me right; a wall thermometer. This is officially what gave her the name "Flava-Flav", as she strongly resembled the celebrity. As if things weren't bad enough, she then was holding one of those huge, canister-style flashlights in one hand. On the other, she had a large, analog tape recorder strapped to her wrist. Steve had the joyous privilege of having Flava-Flav on his team for the investigation. At one point in the night, Steve's EMF meter quit working. However, to Steve's rescue, came Flava-Flav, telling Steve that he could borrow hers. When Steve asked what kind of meter she had, she whips out a freaking volt meter that you use to test the current in wall receptacles. God bless poor ole Flava-Flav, as her arsenal of ghost-hunting weaponry would become the butt of many jokes for years to come.

To this day, the Shreveport Municipal Auditorium continues to draw crowds that are interested in its paranormal history. Haunted nighttime tours are still held there regularly, as well as walking tours around the Ledbetter Heights area, concluding in Oakland Cemetery. Speaking from a paranormal standpoint, our job was complete. We had investigated a historic location that was rumored to contain paranormal activity, bringing back proof of strange occurrences. At the same time, we caused a rise in the curiosity of the building, especially from the paranormal enthusiasts, drawing added tourism from all areas in and around Louisiana. It was a win-win situation by all parties. Now it was time to move on and continue running rampant across the state, offering our investigative services when needed, while educating the public in such an intriguing hobby, proving to everyone that we were a group to be reckoned with.

12

JOSEPH JEFFERSON MANSION (NEW IBERIA, LA)

As I've said time and time again, one of the best things about traveling around the state to investigate various locations is that I get to see some of the most historically-enriched areas that the state has to offer. We all know that we are never guaranteed to have an encounter with a spirit, yet we can always rely on the fact that we will get one hell of a history lesson. Unfortunately, many of these locations represent a dying portion of Louisiana and Cajun culture that many individuals fail to even acknowledge. That is why I am a firm believer in educating others, especially children, on the importance of our Cajun heritage. Despite the several hundred years that various Cajun traditions and languages have been practiced, I fear that my generation will contain the last handful of individuals that are aware of this interesting culture. I regularly teach my young daughter small bits of Cajun French, in the hopes that she may carry on the heritage a little longer. As she gets older, I plan on having her tour some of the historically beautiful locations that I have had the privilege of visiting. Visiting locations such as Oak Alley, San Francisco, Destrehan, Rosedown, and Nottoway Plantations are truly like taking a step back in time. From their lavished landscapes to their intricate internal and external design, you can truly get a personal look at how much things have changed over the years. Personally, I love walking into these homes and immediately smelling the old cypress and cedar used in construction. Up to this point, I had the privilege of investigating numerous plantations and other historical buildings across the state. However, none of these locations had the wide array of history as the next location we would have the opportunity to investigate.

Traveling back for a second to the LGH "Gladiator Days", I can often remember the group leaders mention a home in New Iberia, Louisiana, known as the Joseph Jefferson Mansion. According to them, the location had long been reported to be active, and they were always interested in conducting an investigation there. However, due to their lack of initiative and deformed priorities, no one would ever take the reins and attempt to line up the investigation. LGH was now long gone, and so were their methods of operation. We had a whole new group of dedicated individuals, who constantly looked for new places to investigate. What better place to continue our successful track than the one place that LGH had wanted to investigate for so long. Besides, it would be funny to pour a little salt in the wounds, proving to those that doubted that we could be successful on our own; we were capable of bagging some pretty good investigations.

To give you the best possible introduction on the history of this beautiful home, I must first start with the land that it sits on, known as Jefferson Island. Jefferson Island is located about thirty miles south of Lafayette and makes up a portion of the famous "Five Islands" of Louisiana. The islands were created due to enormous pressures in the earth, forcing large amounts of salt rock from a mother bed located five miles below the earth's surface. This tremendous force elevated several low hills in the coastal areas, forming the Five Islands: Jefferson, Weeks, Belle Isle, Cote Blanche, and Avery Island, which interestingly enough, is the home of Tabasco sauce. These islands are elevated anywhere between fifty to a hundred feet above sea level, with Avery Island being the highest. Due to the islands' distances from the Gulf of Mexico, these elevations are considered to be extremely high, due to them resting on mammoth pockets of salt, said to be about two to three miles wide and up to five miles in depth.

Originally called "Orange Island," Jefferson Island was a Spanish land grant, reported to have fallen into the hands of the brother-in-law of the infamous Jean Lafitte. During Lafitte's reign of terror on the Gulf areas, it is rumored that he often patrolled Bayou Carlin in his shallow-drift pirate boat. The secluded and low-lying waterways were the perfect place for Lafitte to elude captors, such as the law or equally-notorious mercenaries. It is also rumored that the land was also used by Lafitte and his fellow pirates to bury some of their valuable treasure. This would later prove to be more fact than fiction, as in 1923, several pots of Spanish, Mexican, French, and American gold and silver coins were discovered by a Voodoo priest by the name of "Daynight". The treasure was exhumed near one of the massive Oak Trees, said to be over three hundred and fifty years old. After the find, the trees were appropriately nicknamed the Lafitte Oaks.

In 1869, the island was purchased by Joseph Jefferson, the famous nineteenth-century actor who most is known for his performance as Rip Van Winkle in the play based on the writings of Washington Irving. One year after the purchase of the island, Joseph Jefferson built a beautiful twenty-two room mansion with a fourth floor cupola, located on the highest point of the island. The mansion is extremely gorgeous and does not look like most of the homes built during that time period. The styles are quite eclectic, being a mixture of Moorish, Steamboat Gothic, French, and Southern. The front of the property contains massive, centuries-old oak trees and meticulous landscaping. Numerous peacocks roam the grounds, adding an even more illustrious look to the property.

During the many years of Joseph Jefferson's acting career, he obtained a great deal of fame and notoriety, allowing him to befriend many of society's elite. One of his best friends, President Grover Cleveland, visited Jefferson Island on numerous occasions. After a long and productive life, Joseph Jefferson died in 1905, leaving the mansion to his heirs. In 1917, the land was purchased by John Bayless Sr. and eventually handed down to his son, John Jr. John Jr. began to develop an extremely elaborate twenty-acre garden, containing fauna from all over the world. In the 1950's, the Rip Van Winkle Gardens were born, drawing the attention of locals and tourists alike. In 1985, Bayless died and the property was sold in 1996 to Dr. Don Ray. After revitalizing the grounds to their former beauty, it was then sold to Mike Richard of Live Oak Gardens, LTD, in which it is still owned and operated by the father and son duo.

To the rear of the mansion and the gardens, lies Lake Peigneur, an eleven-acre lake that spills into Bayou Carlin mentioned earlier. This lake would be site to one of the strangest natural occurrences in Louisiana history. In November of 1980, due to the land's abundance in oil, gas, and sulphur, a drilling rig was attempting to excavate oil from the lake. It is said that the drilling rig was only six inches off of its targeted mark, yet this slight miscalculation proved to be a huge disaster. The drill bit broke through one of the caverns of the salt dome located beneath the ground. It doesn't take a scientist to know that salt and water don't make a good pair. As water began to run through the small opening of the salt mine, the land began to quickly dissolve, pulling in more and more water. What happened next was unimaginable, as the gaping hole grew to a fifty foot whirlpool, pulling in water, land, century-old trees, and even drilling rigs under the surface into the deep caverns. The enormous erosion caused the largest waterfall in Louisiana history, towering around one hundred and fifty feet. As the crewman of the rigs battled the opposing current of the draining lake, they fought for their lives as they made their way to safety. One eyewitness, who found out the relentlessness and fury of Mother Nature, claimed that he literally thought it was the end of the world. Three hours later, the entire eleven-acre lake was completely drained. Amazingly, there were no casualties, as everyone escaped with their lives.

The scar left behind by this devastating event was a gigantic hole where the lake once stood. In addition, two support pillars are all that is left of the former owner's home. Despite all that had happened, this was not the last of strange events to take place. As current owner, Mike Richard, began digging through the empty lake one day, he was amazed to recover a piece of pre-historic history, in the form of the lower jaw bone and tusks of an ancient Mastodon. Upon further excavation, additional fossils were recovered such as ancient horse teeth and other prehistoric bones. Some of these fossils can still be seen today, along with portions of the recovered buried treasure, in the home's gift shop. Now, the lake has refilled to its former size. What is interesting is that due to the massive amounts of salt still seeping to certain areas of the lake, there are now freshwater and saltwater species of fish in the same body of water.

In addition to a plethora of interesting history that is enough to write a single book about, did I also mention that the place is said to be haunted? Other than a tourist who died of a heart attack on the front porch several years ago, there have never been any other documented deaths on the grounds, yet there have long been reports of strange things taking place here. Visitors and staff of the mansion have reported seeing anomalies ranging from strange green mist along the ceilings to the full-bodied apparition of an elderly man resembling Joseph Jefferson, peering through the second story French windows. The area where the apparition is often seen is said to have been the art studio of Joseph Jefferson, where he would often paint and write. In the front of the property, the sounds of rattling chains and carriages have been heard near the area where the buried treasure had been recovered. In Louisiana folklore, it has often been said that when pirates would bury their treasure, they would often murder one of their own at the site of the burial, serving as a protector over the goods. With such a wide collection of stories, it is still unknown as to where the reported paranormal events have originated from. Whether it is the residual energy from miners years ago, the friendly entity of Joseph Jefferson, or the ghost of an overly-protective pirate, no one truly knows the cause for the strange occurrences at the Joseph Jefferson Mansion.

After I had researched and found such an endless amount of interesting history, I was more determined than ever to obtain access into the mansion. I immediately contacted the owner, Mike, to see if he would allow us to investigate. Amazingly, he immediately returned my call and was more than excited to discuss all of the strange events that have happened on the property. After telling him our request for an investigation, he was more than receptive to the idea and gave us the approval to investigate. It was amazing at how simple it was to get the investigation approved, showing how undetermined LGH was. I then set up a daytime meeting with Mike to conduct a preliminary and to get a look of the beautiful home.

Driving to the property is a task in itself, as it is located deep past Lafayette. The property is located at the end of quarter-mile driveway and is secluded from any traffic or neighbors. Driving up the hill to the home is quite breathtaking, as you instantly see a beautiful, intricately-built home, set on a meticulous lawn that is infested with gorgeous peacocks. I then met with Mike, who was extremely welcoming and hospitable, taking me on a tour of the grounds. In addition to the home, there are also several servant quarters that have been turned into guests' houses. An old building that once served as a school house for the children of the miners now serves as a guest suite. Finally, there is a large restaurant and gift shop on the property.

After speaking with Mike in regards to some of the reported activity that has occurred, he said that, in addition to the main house, people have reported strange occurrences in the restaurant and the guest cottage to the rear of the mansion. During my visit, I had the opportunity to interview one of the house keepers who had previously experienced strange phenomena in the restaurant area. According to the employee, as she was rearranging items in the kitchen area, she witnessed a stack of Styrofoam cups literally shoot out of the plastic sleeve that they were sitting in. They reportedly shot out one at a time, as if being mechanically ejected. A nervous housekeeper quickly left the restaurant, not returning for quite some time.

While touring the main house, I was taken back at the extreme beauty of both the interior and exterior, as both are highly decorated with meticulous detail. I was even more shocked when I learned that when the house was originally purchased by the Bayless family, the home was in such disrepair, there were cows and chickens that freely roamed through the home. Upon further examining, the main entrance serves as a breeze way, allowing warm air to freely circulate up through a hole in all three floors, eventually leading up to the fourth-story cupola. From this amazing viewpoint, you can see all twenty-acres of the gardens, Lake Peigneur, and on a clear day, you can reportedly see a portion of the Gulf of Mexico. On a side note, for you movie enthusiasts, the home was nearly the site for the filming of the movie "The Skeleton Key", however the directors felt that the home was a little too ornate for the theme of the movie. Instead, the movie was filmed at Felicity Plantation, in St. James Parish.

As I continued to walk around the property, I noticed one building that I had not yet explored. The building was equally ornate as the others, yet was embedded in an area that was not kept up quite as much. I noticed that there were shutters on the building, giving the appearance that windows were present, yet upon further examination, it was apparent that the building had none. I made my way to the front of the building and attempted to open the wooden door, only to find out that it was actually a solid steel door with a wooden facade. When I asked Mike the importance of this strangely built building, he advised me that it was actually a bomb shelter that was built by the former owner, who was a little on the eccentric side. Apparently, he was a little edgy during the JFK days of the Cuban Missile Crisis and decided to make a hideout in case things got a little hairy. Sure as all hell, I entered the bunker to find it was constructed of solid slabs of thick concrete. I made it about ten feet into the narrow corridor when I was presented with a huge spider directly in front of my face. As you know by now, that was the furthest I would go into the shelter, as I quickly scurried out of what seemed like a cement fortress. After an extensive introduction of the history-enveloped site, I said my temporary farewells, as I anxiously prepared for the upcoming investigation.

A week had passed and it was now time to conduct the long awaited investigation. We arrived at the mansion around 5:00 PM, to allow everyone to get a good look at the grounds in the day time. We then proceeded to set up three DVR systems: two in the mansion and another in the restaurant. After taking a few random pictures, we then took our base EMF readings, in preparation of the actual investigation. It was in the middle of the summer and none of the air conditioners were turned on that night. As I sweated my ass off, I prayed for a cold spot, whether it be paranormal or not, to grace my presence.

We began the investigation by breaking up into our respective groups and spreading across the large property. Todd and I began by sitting up in the small cupola, which is located on a partial fourth floor, accessible by an extremely steep and narrow spiral staircase. The view was amazing, as we could definitely see out for several miles, looking out under a cloud-free night sky. However, no matter how beautiful the view was, everything seemed to be interrupted by the insatiable heat that was gracing us with its presence that night. For those of you that have never experienced Louisiana heat, you are very lucky. The heat is the number one reason that I prefer ghost hunting during the winter, followed by a close number two, which is that there are no spiders in the winter to contend with. Unfortunately, both would play a role in making for an uneasy investigation.

Later in the evening, I would switch things up a little by partnering up with Brandon. We decided to walk over to the restaurant several hundred yards away from the mansion. The two ways to get to the restaurant were by either taking the gravel driveway from the mansion to the restaurant, or taking the longer route, which was through a portion of the twenty-acre gardens. As you can guess, we couldn't do anything simple, as we opted for the longer route. Something should have rang a bell when we saw a huge display map, instructing us on the proper routes to take in order to exit the gardens, since they were literally a maze. Still, the men in us figured we didn't need any sort of directions, so we decided to just wing it. I was equipped with an extremely bright two million candle power spotlight. However, the con was that the light drained so much power, I only had about fifteen minutes of battery use so we really didn't have any time to waste in making it from the mansion to the restaurant.

We began walking through the darkened maze, passing endless species of plants that contained tons of flowers, fruits, and vegetables. About ten minutes into the stroll, Brandon came to an abrupt stop, as if he had just heard something. After asking him why he stopped so suddenly, Brandon stated that he thought that he heard what sounded like footsteps behind us. After I also stopped to see if I could hear something as well, I began to hear the faint sound of what sounded like feet scuffling through the bushes. I panned my spotlight in all directions, trying to find the source of the noise, yet I was unsuccessful. I wasted so much time trying to find the sound's origin; I noticed that the light had begun to start dimming. I knew that we only had about five minutes left of light, before we would be forced to find our way out of the gardens with only a small pocket flashlight.

As we walked a few more feet, it seemed as if the footsteps were getting louder and louder. As the pace of our own feet picked up, so did those of our unseen admirer. Once again, Brandon came to a complete halt, as he nervously said, "Where is that noise coming from?" Just as he said that, it sounded as though whatever was near us began to charge in our direction. I focused my quickly-dimming spotlight towards the section of bushes where the commotion was coming from. Suddenly, the largest damn armadillo I have ever seen in my life emerged from the bushes and ran straight between Brandon's legs, causing him to briefly stumble. In one of the most pathetic defensive moves I have ever seen, Brandon let out the most feminine squeal imaginable, balled up his fists, and squared off like a heavyweight boxer. To this day, I have no clue as to whether or not he got into that hilarious fighting stance out of instinct, or he actually thought he was going to go round for round with a freaking armadillo. Regardless of his intentions, I immediately broke out into an uncontrollable laughter, as the look on his face was simply priceless. Unfortunately, my lack of sympathy would soon come back to bite me in the butt. I was in such a fit of laughter; I had no clue that I had run right smack into a huge spider web. As the strands of the web wrapped around by head and face, I quickly went into an instant panic, flailing my hands in all directions. It truly felt that I had hundreds of spiders now crawling over me, as I continued to panic more and more. Our antics could have easily been those seen in a comedy, as the two of us were freaking out for no valid reason. What we had failed to realize was that during our heroic antics, we had scrambled around so much that we had taken the wrong path through the maze-like gardens and were now completely lost, as our spotlight was now pretty much completely dim. After about thirty minutes of stumbling through wooded area, illuminated only by the light from a small pocket-size flashlight that we were now forced to use, we finally made our way out of the gardens. Needless to say, this was the last time that we would take the safari route.

Besides our little displays of masculinity and our encounters with nature, nothing else substantial occurred in regards to first hand experiences that night. After recording approximately six hours of video and audio from several devices, we concluded our investigation. Fortunately, the owner was kind enough to allow us to spend the night in several of the adjacent cottages, which were extremely nice. The next morning, we loaded up all of our equipment and made the long drive home. I always hate the day following an investigation, due to the fact that you never get to sleep in and by the time you finally make it back home, you are more exhausted than if you would have just drove straight home that night. Just a few of the sacrifices a ghost hunter makes.

As it came time to review the video and audio obtained, I knew we had a task ahead of us, as we had three separate DVR systems to review, all of which contained video from four separate cameras. Despite the enormous size of the buildings, we tried our best to cover all the areas that seemed to be the focus points for activity. The one area that I wanted to focus the most on was the former art studio of Joseph Jefferson, located on the second floor of the mansion. The room contained two large French windows, which faced the rear of the property. As mentioned earlier, these were the same windows that eyewitnesses have reported seeing an elderly man, resembling Joseph Jefferson, peering from left to right out of the windows. Based on the past eyewitness accounts, I decided to place one camera on the inside of the study, looking directly out of the double French windows. I would have never imagined that my specific camera placement would have paid off.

While reviewing the video, I noticed a very interesting anomaly. At the bottom left hand corner of the screen, I noticed what appeared to simply be a particle of dust. Normally, I would not have given the orb-like object a second look; however there was something quite unique about its flight pattern. The object floated up to the right panel of the French windows and stopped in mid air. It then floated to the left panel, paused, returned to the right panel, paused again, and then suddenly flew off the right side of the screen. I was immediately amazed at the specific flight pattern of this object, as it truly seemed to have a mind of its own. There were definitely no strange air currents on the second floor that night, as I can strongly remember that the air conditioner was not working that night and I sweated my butt off. In regards to the anomaly possibly being an insect, I highly doubt it, as I have never seen any type of insect with such a fluid movement. What was most interesting is that the flight pattern of the object strongly resembled the previous reports of witnessing an unknown elderly man, peeking out of each of the French windows. To this day, the strange anomaly captured at the Joseph Jefferson mansion would still be one of my favorite pieces of evidence that I have collected.

To this day, I have looked forward to revisiting the mansion to conduct a follow-up investigation. There is just way too much history and questionable events involving the mansion to simply walk off with one interesting video clip and claim that all of the previous reports to be inconclusive. After the initial investigation, I now looked to broaden my investigation resume, so to speak, by considering locations other than the traditional grand plantation on acres of manicured lawns. I decided to expand by now looking into locations that were more affiliated to places that were similar to locations that I could relate to. Due to my years in a corrections environment, there was no better place to look at than some sort of jail or prison.

13
DERIDDER GOTHIC JAIL (DERIDDER, LA)

I have always been fascinated with being a policeman ever since I was a young child. Growing up, I can remember religiously watching CHIPS, with the dreams of one day becoming a policeman. I would equip myself with my cap guns, gloves, and helmet, as I rode around on my rechargeable motorcycle, mimicking the actions of the television stars. As I prepared to graduate from high school, I was certain that I wanted to major in Criminal Justice, and ultimately become a Louisiana State Trooper. As I mentioned earlier, after a year of college I decided to get a little experience under my belt, so I became a Sheriff's Deputy for Avoyelles Parish. I was assigned to the night shift of the booking office, which would end up being the most enjoyable job I have ever had. During my short three years in the booking office, I have seen some of the most hilarious things one can possibly imagine. The most enjoyable times were normally the Saturday nights, when all of the drunks and weirdoes would get brought in once the bars were closed down. I can remember trying my best not to laugh as the half-dressed, drunk women stumbled into the jail, as they cried and pleaded that they were innocent, offering everything from money to sex, just so they could get out of jail. Oh, how those were the days.

Gears quickly shifted as I became employed with the Federal Bureau of Prisons. I had now left an enjoyable, often humorous, job to work at what would soon become one of the most violent maximum security prisons in the Federal system. Working in a penitentiary is truly an experience, as you unfortunately see a side of mankind that very few people will ever see. On a daily basis, I sadly see more evil than most people see in a lifetime. It is an unfortunate truth that seeing these acts on a daily basis definitely takes a toll on you, hardening you up to a degree that can often affect your home life. Regularly seeing severe assaults, murders, and other violent acts causes one to often acquire what is known as gallow-humor, which desensitizes you so much, you begin to find humor in some of the most violent and grotesque acts. This can often cause problems when associating with non-law enforcement friends. I have often made crude jokes or taken serious events lightly, offending others that simply do not understand that the things they find terrible are things that I deal with on a regular basis.

My years of interest and involvement in prison systems have definitely carried over into my interest in the paranormal. If the theory is true that most hauntings are due to violent and untimely deaths, then jails and prisons would definitely be on the top of the list for being haunted. As mentioned earlier, infamous prisons such as Angola State Penitentiary, Alcatraz, and Eastern State Penitentiary are notorious for reportedly containing their share of paranormal activity. Whether it is due to the intense violence or the overall large amount of negative energy, it would only be suiting that these places would not only be haunted, but contain some of the more unfriendly spirits around.

As my list of investigations lengthened, I continued to have an interest for investigating a potentially haunted jail or prison. By this time, we had investigated homes, restaurants, bars, plantations, hair salons, town halls, and hotels, although we had yet to get the opportunity to visit a jail. I began doing intense research on unused jails in Louisiana that were rumored to be haunted. During my search, I continued hearing about a jail in Shreveport, known as the Pea Farm, which was built at the turn of the century, ultimately closing down in the 1950's. Legends are that the Pea Farm housed some of the more violent offenders of the time and was home to numerous murders and assaults. The jail is often visited by high school kids, who only add to the haunted stories. Those who have visited the jail have reported hearing screams and pleas for help, although many of these reports may simply be your standard urban legends.

Although I had an interest to investigate the Pea Farm, I was uncertain as to if I wanted to go through the trouble. The jail was located deep in the wooded area of a not so reputable portion of Shreveport and I did not feel like battling both spirits and crack heads on any given night. In addition, I had spoke with several individuals who had visited the jail and they all stated that, despite the eerie look of the jail, they felt that all of the haunted reports were merely local legends. With the cons outweighing the pros, I decided that it would not be feasible to attempt a thorough investigation of an abandoned jail with no electricity, located in an unfavorable part of town. I decided to scratch my attempts of investigating the Pea Farm and began looking for other interesting locations.

At the time, one of our members was once part of a small investigative group out of Beauregard Parish. The group was a small, local faction that primarily investigated cemeteries. My member mentioned of an abandoned jail that was located in that parish and was known as the Deridder Gothic Jail. For years, this local group had attempted to gain access into this jail, which had been reported to be haunted for quite some time. However, their requests would fall on deaf ears, as their attempts were to no avail, leaving the jail untouched. However, I am a firm believer in "one man's meat is another man's poison", so I decided to conduct my own research on the jail and see if it was worthy of an investigation.

Initially, I was simply shown a photograph of the jail, which immediately surprised me. I had seen many jails and prisons in my life, yet I had never seen one so eye-appealing. In an instant, I was reminded why the structure was called Gothic, as every inch of the jail mimicked Gothic characteristics. With its arches over the windows and main entrance, as well as several false corner buttresses, a design like this was more likely to have been seen at a college, not a jail. The building consisted of three stories with a fourth-floor tower that overlooked a very unique block of town. Ironically, on this one block, there was a jail, courthouse, post office, and school, accommodating to a wide array of society, to say the least. It is said that the ornateness of the jail is primarily due to its proximity to the adjacent courthouse, which are similar in appearance. Interestingly enough, the two buildings are connected by an underground tunnel, which would aid in the secure transport of inmates directly from the jail, through the tunnel, and up a secure rear stairwell that led directly into the courtroom.

The jail was built in 1914 and was used in housing local inmates until 1984. The building, extremely ornate in fashion, was said to be able to hold just over one hundred inmates in its three story structure. This seemed hard to believe, as the jail did not look that large, despite being three stories tall. During its seventy years of operation, the jail would probably be best known for its double hangings, which took place on March 9, 1928.

On August 28, 1926, Louisiana natives Joe Genna and Milton Brasseaux committed one of the most heinous crimes in the state's history, when they brutally murdered Deridder taxi driver, J.J. Brevelle. The two men coaxed Brevelle into driving them to a remote spot in eastern Beauregard Parish. Once there, the plan went terribly wrong, as Brevelle was severely beaten with a tire iron, stabbed in the head, and finally had his throat slashed. After getting away with only fourteen dollars, the two men disposed of the body in an old mill pond in Pickering, Louisiana, and fled the scene in Brevelle's taxi, which was later found abandoned and burned in Calcasieu Parish.

On September 2, 1926, after a short, yet successful, manhunt, the two men were arrested; Genna in Orange, Texas, and Brasseaux, in Sulphur, Louisiana. Six days after their arrest, the jury indicted the two men. On December 11, 1926, both men were sentenced to death by hanging. An interesting feature of the jail was that it contained a spiral stair case that led all the way to the third floor. From the first floor, one could look straight up and see a barred opening, looking into the ornamental tower. It is this barred opening that would serve as the execution site, with the aid of makeshift gallows, constructed on the third floor. Executioners would simply escort the inmate up the gallows and fasten a noose around their neck, which was then secured to the bars above their heads. One can only imagine the psychological effect caused by looking up from the first floor, witnessing the inmate fight for his life as he dangled from the ceiling.

It is rumored that the jail was quite popular for its hangings over the years, often serving as entertainment for the local community. It is even said that the adjacent school would often dismiss early, just so people of all ages could witness the town's justice system being served. This is all a bit ironic, especially due to the fact that the town of Deridder is located directly in the bible belt of Louisiana. It is rumored that for the town's size, it actually holds an unverifiable record for having the most churches per capita.

After several failed attempts at appeals, the two men were scheduled to be executed on March 9, 1928. The week leading up to the event, one of the men tried to speed up the process by attempting suicide with no success. As scheduled, both men were escorted from their isolated cells on the third floor and briskly walked to the nearby gallows, only several feet away. As instructed by the State of Louisiana, both men were promptly sentenced to death by hanging. This would eventually be one of the last "legal" hangings carried out by the State of Louisiana, as this form of execution would be overridden in 1941 by the electric chair.

The infamous double hangings would not be the only dark days reported at the Deridder Gothic Jail. The jail would also be home to several other deaths by means of suicide and natural causes. In one noteworthy case, there was a severe assault that took place in one of the cells on the second floor. According to former staff, the cell contained an inmate with a long sentence for murder and an inmate that was simply a street arrest. For whatever strange reasons the two inmates with such different statuses were celled together, an altercation ensued between the two. The convicted murderer removed a portion of a window frame and brutally beat the other inmate unconscious. Although the inmate was not killed in the beating, he was literally left brain dead, never recovering from the onslaught.

As you can imagine, a place with such a dark history would inevitably be reported as being potentially active. According to former staff of the jail, as well as current city employees, the jail has long been the home to strange occurrences such as phantom voices and reports of apparitions. In one interesting case, a photographer was taking professional shots of the jail for display purposes. When the film was developed, an anomaly appeared on the front porch, resembling the figure of an elderly man. The description strongly matches those given by other eyewitnesses over the years. The man is said to have white hair, smoking a pipe or cigar, and is seen dressed in what appears to be either maintenance clothing or an old jailor's uniform.

I was now more interested than ever to try and obtain permission to investigate the jail. Looking at how many failed attempts the other group had, I was somewhat hesitant to make the initial contact. No one ever likes to be denied an investigation, yet you won't know until you at least try. I was uncertain as to whom exactly I needed to contact, but after seeing a website that mentioned the Beauregard Tourist Commission in correlation to the jail, I decided to try them first. I initially sent one of our detailed investigation request letters, letting the tourist committee know my reasons for writing. To my surprise, I was contacted only days later from Lori Veazy, Director of the tourist committee. Based on her e-mail, she seemed extremely willing to entertain the idea of allowing us to investigate. I immediately thought that this was too good to be true, as it all seemed way too easy. As I said, this other group had tried for years, or so they claim, and all I did was send a simple e-mail and things were already looking promising.

Lori stated that despite the fact that she was extremely interested in having us, she was still not the decisive factor. The request would have to be brought in front of the police jury, during one of their monthly meetings and they would have to take a vote on whether or not we could investigate. Even though their next meeting would not be for another two weeks, I asked Lori if I could still meet with her to look around the jail during the day, in which she gladly agreed.

I made the hour and a half drive from Alexandria to the "rocking" town of Deridder. It is quite amusing to drive through Deridder due to the fact that as "holy rolly" as most of the town acts, there appears to be a strip club and/or a tattoo parlor every fifty feet. For all of you that are ever traveling through central Louisiana and are in desperate need of a tattoo, lap dance, or Chinese buffet, Deridder is the place to visit.

I arrived at the jail and was immediately surprised at how eye-appealing the place was. The building would have made for a beautiful private home, much less a jail and an execution site. I was also surprised at the size of the jail, which definitely didn't look like it was capable of holding one hundred inmates. I then met with an extremely friendly Lori, who was quite excited about the whole potential project. We began the walkthrough by entering the jail through a side opening, which was completely unprotected from visitors. Lori advised that this was often a problem, as they would regularly find homeless people camping out in the jail. The first room we entered was the area that once served as the holding cell for local arrests off the street. The room simply consisted of a large metal grating, dividing the room in half, a toilet, and a desk area to perform the booking process. Exiting the holding cell area, I was taken back as I saw the large spiral staircase that led all the way to the third floor, exposing the barred roof opening where the executions were once carried out. As I looked up, I could not help but imagine an individual swinging from that height, and what type of deterrent that must have served for spectators.

The staircase also served as an access port to the tunnel that connected the jail to the courthouse. As I walked down the steps, I immediately felt a change in temperature, as I was now entering a dark and damp area that was made entirely of concrete. The tunnel was quite long, making three ninety degree turns, spanning out several hundred feet. At the end of the tunnel were several steps that led to an extremely steep set of stairs that covered all three floors of the court house. Once we made the tiring climb, there was a very small door, approximately three feet tall. Once I opened the door, I realized that we had actually made our way to the roof of the courthouse, giving an impressive look of the town. As I mentioned, the entire construction was ingenious, as inmates could be securely transported from the jail to the actual courtroom without ever being seen by the public.

Returning to the jail, we came up to the area that once served as the kitchen. Being no bigger than a home kitchen, it was obvious that the inmates were required to eat in their cells. In the kitchen was actually a small "dummy waiter" that was actually used to transport food trays to the second and third floors. The trays were placed in the small compartment and, by pulling a rope, the platform would be raised to the appropriate floor.

Ascending to the second and third floors, we had now entered the area that contained the jail cells. The layout of the jail is quite unique, as its design can be described as a flowered pattern. The center of the floor is open due to the spiral staircase, and there are rooms at each of the four corners. Each room is secured with a heavy steel door and a barred grill that must be manually opened with a key. On the second floor, there was one room that appeared to be for general population inmates, as there were twelve bunk beds still in place, along with a toilet, sink, and shower. One can only begin to imagine the tension involving twelve men and one toilet. Next, two of the four rooms consisted of an open bay area that appearing to once be able to hold two to three inmates. The fourth cell was known as the "death cell" and was basically an isolation area. In the room itself, there was a large caged area that was divided into two. In each section there was a bunk and an extremely small toilet and sink. To access each small compartment, there was a two-door "sally port" system, which enabled the jailors to securely place the inmate back in his cell, while safely removing his restraints. As I made my way to the third floor, I noticed that the room layouts were identical as to the second floor.

As I wandered through the jail, I could not help but place myself back in time when the jail was in operation. As I sat on one of the rusted bunk beds, I looked around at the paint-peeled walls, reading the graffiti and wall carvings still visible from years ago. In each profane-induced note, I tried to put myself in that inmate's shoes, wondering what he had done to be put in jail. I sat back on the bed as I could mentally hear the rattling of keys and slamming of grills, imagining what the walls would say if they could actually talk. While we were upstairs, I could hear sounds coming from the first floor, as if someone was walking around. As we descended the stairs, we were greeted by a man and his wife who were simply sightseeing. The man appeared to be in his late fifties and stated that he once spent the night in the holding cell area back in the seventies because of a DWI charge. After asking him a few questions about how the jail looked, we had a few laughs and the couple was on their way.

I thanked Lori for giving me a tour of the jail and we discussed what would be needed to present our request to the police jury. Unfortunately, I would not be able to attend the actual meeting, so I decided to have one of my members at the time make the formal request during the town's monthly meeting. We were all weary as to how the police jury would react to our request, so I was more certain than ever that we present our self as a group that conducted skeptical investigations and were not a group of weirdoes.

The evening of the meeting came and we presented our formal request to the police jury. Luckily, we had the support of Lori, who had also attended the meeting and gave her recommendations on our behalf. Amazingly, in a unanimous vote, the police jury approved our request to investigate the jail. I could not believe that we would now be the first group allowed in the jail, after others had tried and failed for so long. The simple fact that we were chosen over others ensured me that we were well on our way to being known as a reputable group. Our mission statements, presentation abilities, and people skills were now fine tuned and we could now be seen as a legitimate group in a field of so many embarrassments.

Another individual that was present at the meeting was Shawn Martin, a reporter for a major newspaper in Lake Charles. Shawn was already interested in the paranormal and, ironically, had worked at the Deridder Gothic Jail before it closed down in 1984. When he heard of our request to investigate the jail, he immediately wrote a story for his paper, giving an in-depth history of the jail as well as our group. The article had mixed reviews, as many of the bible-pounding town locals immediately thought we were a bunch of devil worshipers. They began calling the newspaper and the police jury with the concerns that we were going to camp out on the town square with Ouija boards and perform all kinds of crazy rituals. In one humorous call, the concerned citizen expressed the belief that we were going to bring in drugs into the community. In a very clever rebuttal, Shawn said, "Mam, if you would see a majority of the people in the town, it's safe to say that drugs have already been here for quite some time."

Once we had obtained permission to investigate the jail, one issue that crossed my mind was the local group that had tried to obtain access to the jail for so long. Despite what many may say, I do have quite a conscious and I actually felt bad that after their many failed attempts, we had succeeded after the first try. A problem with many groups is that they become extremely territorial and get upset when a group from another area enters their "turf" to conduct an investigation in their area. I find the whole concept quite ridiculous, especially due to the fact that it's not like any given group can truly stake claims or ownership of an investigation site. However, I have seen many groups become quite hostile if someone else investigates an area that they feel they should have sole reign over. In one pathetic example, a small group here in Louisiana investigated a certain plantation home. They went on and on about how they were promised that they would be the only ones ever allowed investigating it. Despite their futile claims, another group from Louisiana also was granted permission to investigate the same plantation. Within weeks of the approval, the first group contacted the plantation owner for some unknown reason. It is unknown as to what was said to the owner, but when the second group contacted him, he now had a complete change of heart, saying that he no longer wanted them to investigate and did not give them a reason why. Again, these are just some of the dirty tactics that some groups will resort to. To me, it is completely idiotic as to what these individuals think they are accomplishing when they stoop to such low levels. Unfortunately, I would be a first hand witness to these antics on many more occasions.

With my conscious still weighing on me in regards to the other group, I decided to offer out an olive branch, so to speak. I knew that I would not have the room to accommodate our group and the other entire group to simultaneously investigate the jail, so I contacted the group's founder and told him that he was more than welcome to investigate with us. Since I knew that the jail was on his wish list for so long, I felt that it would be only right to give him the opportunity to investigate with us. He was immediately elated, instantly taking me up on my offer. I further advised him that he was able to stay as long as he wanted and could investigate in any fashion that he wished. See, I can be a nice guy sometimes.

The day of the investigation had finally arrived. I was extremely excited due to the fact that not only we were investigating the jail; we had also decided that we would spend the night in the actual cells while we left our cameras recording. With it being November, we made sure to bring plenty of sleeping bags and space heaters, since the jail was extremely drafty and cold. We arrived at the jail around 4:00 PM and were greeted by Shawn and Lori, who was there to watch us briefly set up then leave, as they had no urges to spend the night with us.

Our attention immediately drew to the open doorway on the side of the jail. We were worried that this would pose a threat during the investigation, as anyone could literally come in the jail without us knowing. Our ingenuity quickly kicked in, as Todd made a quick run to a local hardware store. He returned with a large sheet of plywood, several pieces of hardware, and a padlock. Within thirty minutes, Todd constructed a makeshift door that we could actually lock. The door would not only keep us protected during the night, it would also prevent future loitering from the homeless and nosey individuals. Not to brag, but there aren't many investigative groups out there that would do something like that for the client.

Once we insured our safety for the evening, we began to setup our equipment, which consisted of three DVR systems and a total of sixteen IR cameras. We would set up our monitoring station in the front office area, with all the video cables running up through the center opening of each floor, spreading out to each appropriate cell. We quickly learned that going over the video was going to be a pain simply because there was so much dust in the entire building; every screen looked like a disco party was going on. We then began taking our base EMF readings, finding out that the entire building was pretty neutral, with base readings no higher than .3 millagauss.

Prior to the investigation, we were also accompanied by a news reporter with a television station out of Lake Charles. He was to simply film a story on our investigation, briefly following us as we performed a mock investigation for the camera. Around 10:00 PM, the reporter followed Brandon and I into one of the "death cells" on the second floor. After a few minutes of interviewing us in regards to our interests in the jail, he briefly filmed us as we mimicked EMF sweeps. As we walked out of the cell, Brandon began to record several substantial EMF spikes. Everyone continued walking, as Brandon lagged behind to find the source of the unexplainable increased in electromagnetic energy. As the spikes dissipated and Brandon began to walk off, the tripod and IR camera that was next to him simply fell over. This was an extremely sturdy tripod that had been holding the camera all night. We decided to rewind the video to see if possibly Brandon had accidentally bumped into the camera or got tangled up in the video cable. After reviewing the video, it was apparent that the camera fell over when Brandon was several feet away from it. In addition, as the camera was falling, you can see that there was about three feet of slack remaining in the cable, proving that Brandon didn't trip up in the cords either. Although the occurrence was quite interesting, we were unable to officially label it as a paranormal event. Even though we knew that the tripod was extremely sturdy, the simple fact that there was the possibility that it fell over due to being improperly set up, we must write the event off as explainable.

Throughout the entire night, the founder of the other group conducted his own little investigation. He seemed quite please, thanking me numerous times for allowing him to investigate with us. His main compliment was how impressed he was with the extensive amount of equipment we used. He stated that he had always been a fan of using minimal equipment and going strictly on senses, yet after seeing how we investigated, he was now interested in obtaining his own DVR setup and following a more scientific approach. Prior to calling it a night, I offered the founder of the other group to stay with us until the morning, however he declined, and decided to head home, once again thanking us for allowing him to attend. It really made me feel good when I saw that we were able to give the guy a chance to investigate a place that he had dreamed of visiting for so long.

The rest of the night was pretty uneventful, as no other firsthand experiences were reported. We all camped out in one of the open bay cells, while audio and video recorders continued to run. The next morning, we packed up all of our equipment and made our way back home with hours of evidence to go over.

Unfortunately, the entire investigation was not as productive as I would have hoped for, yet I was still elated to have finally investigated an abandoned jail, not to mention, one that was so unique. The only hard piece of evidence we collected was when another member and I were sitting in one of the isolation cells. As the two of us are talking, you can hear a very clear third-party say, "No." The walls were extremely dense and there was no one else near that could have caused the voice.

Several days later, we were rewarded with several media acknowledgments, courtesy of the Lake Charles newspaper and television station. In addition, we were honored with a very well-written story courtesy of Hattie Sherrick with Deridder's local newspaper. As with our other events, our professional approach had once again allowed us to receive extremely positive media recognition, which ultimately put a stop to all the concerned locals that thought we were a bunch of devil-worshipers.

However, as the old saying goes: "If it's not bedbugs, it's piss ants." A week or so after the articles were printed; I received a call from one of the news reporters. Apparently, for the last several days, she had been receiving calls from the founder of the local group that we had allowed to investigate with us. According to the reporter, the guy constantly belittled us, saying how rude we were to him during the night. He even went as far as saying that when he arrived at the jail, I told him that he was going to do exactly what I told him to do and when he questioned this, I told him to, "sit down and shut up." I was absolutely flabbergasted, especially after I had gone completely out of my way to include him in an event that I had no obligation to fulfill.

Of course, with the personality that I have, I immediately contacted the individual to see if this was all true. As with anybody of his caliber, he immediately began to nervously deny everything, putting his foot in his mouth every step of the way. This obviously infuriated me, as I was quick to truly let him know what I thought of ungrateful individuals such as him. There is nothing that upsets me more than when you try and do something nice for someone and they spit in your face. Fortunately, this would only prepare me for a much larger display of deceitfulness later on down the road, which I will get to later.

Just when I thought that such an unnecessary incident had finally passed, I would occasionally catch numerous snide remarks on message boards and blogs, courtesy of the same guy, indirectly bad mouthing groups that approached things from the same scientific standpoint that we did. Ultimately, his actions would go ignored, which is often the best way to handle such stupidity. By turning the other cheek and refusing to stoop to their level, you show that you are a much better person and that reputation will reflect in the quality of your work. For a while, they even tried a ridiculous tactic of conducting follow-up investigations of places we had investigated and found no evidence at. Miraculously, when they would investigate the same location, they would discover tons of "evidence". Whether or not this was an attempt to try and show they were better because they obtained evidence when we didn't, it was absolutely absurd for someone to actually go to such lengths to prove domination.

I still cannot believe why so many people feel that this is a competition. People start watching various television shows that contain normal people that lucked up, getting their own paranormal show, and now they feel that they can do the same thing. Even if hopes of stardom are not the primary goal, I still find it strange that there is such a lack of unity amongst groups. I have been to numerous paranormal conferences and seminars where multiple groups gather and offer different opinions on the hobby. What I have always found hard to believe is that with any type of social conference, everyone quickly becomes a close-knit group, all sharing stories in whatever hobby they are interested in. With paranormal gatherings, I notice that groups quickly begin to isolate themselves from others, forming little cliques amongst one another. As I mentioned, maybe it is due to the fact that there are so many subcategories in the paranormal, there tends to be a much wider range of beliefs than with other hobbies. Just as with questions such as, "Who killed Kennedy," the answer to why there is so much animosity in ghost hunting continues to remain a mystery.

Now that the bulk of the headache had subsided, we continued to press on with our investigations. As with the Shreveport Municipal Auditorium, we would ultimately bring quite a bit of curiosity to the jail. We would later conduct a follow-up investigation, recovering a very interesting audio clip of a male voice that says, "Warden." A year or so later, we would even begin offering group investigations for the public, as part of our continuing education courses that would later become a huge hit with numerous universities across the state.

I continue to regularly speak with Lori and other members of the tourist committee in reference to the jail. For quite some time, they have made attempts to obtain grants to deservingly restore the jail to its original appearance, transforming it into a museum. Fortunately, with the added attention we have brought upon the building, the tourist committee is now closer than ever in receiving all of the funds needed to carry out the appropriate restorations. I would absolutely love to see the jail restored and turned into a museum, not only to see a piece of Louisiana history live on, but to have the self-affirmation to say that I may have had something to do with the completion of the project.

Investigations now began to literally pour in at a record rate, as we continued to receive positive acknowledgment from the media and the community. We would continue to partake in small speaking engagements, educating the public in the proper ways to conduct paranormal investigations in order to be taken seriously. Up to this point, we had only conducted investigations in Louisiana, and we were know looking at taking some sort of large road trip to investigate one of the many reportedly haunted locations throughout the country. We knew that if we were going to spend so much time and money on this out-of-state investigation, we had to be sure that we investigated one of the more infamous locations known. Little did I know that I would soon be conducting the most intense investigation I would ever be involved in, proving once again, be careful what you wish for, because you just might get it. In addition, I would also learn the valuable lesson that just when you think you have seen the lowest forms of deceitfulness from people that you have helped and thought were legitimate friends; someone will always cease to amaze you.

14
WAVERLY HILLS TUBERCULOSIS SANATORIUM (LOUISVILLE, KY)

With everything that the group had now been through, it was safe to say that we were well on our way to becoming the most reputable and widely-accepted group in Louisiana. We had been featured on countless paranormal radio programs and featured in a great deal of paranormal and non-paranormal publications. Cases were now pouring in from all across the state. As with anything, too much of the same thing starts to get monotonous so we decided to take a road trip to investigate one of the many supposedly haunted locations across the country. Trying to pick a location that everyone wanted to investigate was like pulling teeth. Everyone wanted to go somewhere different. Notorious places such as Eastern State Penitentiary in Pennsylvania, St. Augustine Lighthouse in Florida, the Crescent Hotel in Arkansas, and the Winchester House in California were all among the top of the requested location sites. However, no place drew more curiosity from the group than the famous Waverly Hills Tuberculosis Sanatorium in Louisville, Kentucky, said to be one of the most haunted locations in the country.

Waverly Hills Tuberculosis Sanatorium was built in 1910 and was originally a two-story wooden structure, erected to treat tuberculosis patients in the local area. It received its name from a small school that was located in the area, named after the Walter Scott's Waverley novels. At the time, the hospital was only capable of treating forty to fifty patients at a time. With a massive outbreak of TB arriving in 1911, the hospital decided to expand to treat more patients. After adding on several more pavilions, the hospital was now treating approximately one hundred and thirty patients. As the number of cases continued the rise, so did the need for additional bed space. In March 1924, construction began on a massive five-story hospital that would be able to treat more than four hundred patients. The hospital was opened on October 17, 1926, and was the grandest and most sophisticated TB hospitals of its time. The hospital was in operation until June of 1961 and was then reopened the following year as Woodhaven Geriatrics Hospital. Controversially, the hospital was then closed for good in 1981, due to rumored reports of cruelty to the infirmed.

To truly understand the severity of TB, one must look at its origin. Tuberculosis was officially discovered in 1882 by a German physician named Robert Koch, however, traces of TB can be found in Egyptian mummies dating as far back as 4,000 BC. TB is an infectious disease caused by deadly pathogens formed by mycobacteria. The disease most commonly affects the lungs and respiratory system, but can also affect the central nervous system, circulatory system, and lymphatic system. The disease is normally transmitted through saliva and actions such as coughing, sneezing, or spitting. The first symptoms of TB are severe chest pains and the coughing up of blood. If left untreated, TB can easily cause respiratory distress, ultimately leading to death. So was the case with the hundreds of thousands of individuals that died from the deadly plague that ravaged the United States in the early 1900's.

With swift detection methods and modern treatment, TB is treated quite easily in the present day. However, years ago, no one knew of legitimate treatments, often causing medical staff to generate strange and unorthodox methods of treatment that would cause more harm than good. One of these unusual treatments was known as a Pneumothorax, which involved the intentional collapsing of one of the lungs. The theory behind this was that by deflating the lung, it would allow the infected portion to heal while not in use. In cases where the damaged portion was too far gone, a Lobectomy was performed, removing the unneeded piece of lung.

One of the least used and most dangerous treatments was known as a Thoracoplasty. This procedure consisted of removing up to seven or eight of the patient's ribs, allowing the lungs to further expand, taking in a larger amount of fresh air. As one can imagine, this was an extremely life threatening procedure, having only a five percent survival rate. However, due to the fatalness of TB, those infected were willing to try any and all possible treatments available.

The two most commonly used forms of treatment would actually prove later to be the most beneficial. Simple overexposure to fresh, chilled air greatly benefited TB patients, as the clean air was later found to remove the harmful bacteria from the lungs. The other treatment was known as Heliotherapy, and was simply exposure to the hot sun. When the patients were exposed to the hot sun for long periods of time, it served as a bactericide, killing the TB-causing bacteria that caused the disease.

The proof that these methods were widely used at Waverly Hills is apparent in its construction. On the first four floors on the rear side, there are large solariums that go from one end of the hospital to the other. These solariums had no windows, allowing large amounts of fresh air to constantly circulate throughout the building. The patients' rooms led directly into the solariums, allowing their beds to simply be rolled out to the open areas to take in the fresh air. The solariums were used year round, even in the winter months. The fifth floor was only a partial floor; so much of the roof was exposed. The roof area was also used for Heliotherapy purposes, as the young children who were housed on the fifth floor was literally brought out to play in no more than their underwear, simply to get fresh air and absorb large amounts of sunlight.

Despite the many attempts at treatment, there is no shying away from the fact that thousands died from the deadly disease. For years, that have been debates on how many deaths actually took place at Waverly Hills. Personally, I have heard numbers ranging from sixty thousand to over a hundred thousand, yet many feel that those numbers are actually state-wide figures. Regardless, thousands did in fact die at the hospital, making it a prime location for possible paranormal activity.

Adjacent to the hospital is what is known as the death tunnel, which is a massive concrete tunnel, approximately five hundred feet in length. The tunnel sits at a forty-five degree angle and was constructed to allow workers to quickly move goods from the hospital to the awaiting railroad at the base of the tunnel. Half of the tunnel contains steps, while the other half is a smooth ramp that once held a motorized rail and cable system. It is reported that the tunnel was also used to discreetly transport the thousands of deceased individuals in a fashion that would not affect the patients' already low morale.

In addition to the possibly exaggerated death toll, there are several other myths that encompass the hospital. One of the most often mentioned is the legend of room 502. According to folklore, room 502 was home to a suicide of one of the nurses at the time, Mary Hillenburg. It is said that she killed herself due to the fact that she was pregnant with a child out of wedlock. However, two interesting pieces of information lead many to think that the story is simply legend. First, room 502 is actually a restroom and contained no large light fixtures that could have supported a person. Second, there were only two reported deaths of people with the last name "Hillenburg" and they actually took place after Waverly Hills had closed.

Another one of the infamous legends of Waverly Hills is the existence of the "draining room." Tales tell that the room was used to drain the deceased patients of any and all infected fluids prior to transporting them through the death tunnel, ultimately making their bodies lighter to haul off. The bodies were said to have been hung from their feet, at which time they were cut open from the sternum to the groin, allowing all of the fluids to drain out. In actuality, in both sets of mechanical drawings from 1924 and 1962, the room reported to be the draining room is actually labeled as a transformer room. The room has, what appear to be, openings in the walls that were used to house wiring and other electrical equipment. Finally, it is commonly known that procedures such as this would not have been carried out in a hospital setting. If anything similar in nature was to take place, it would have definitely occurred once the body was handed over to the coroner.

Regardless of all the rumored tales of Waverly Hills, the truth is that it is home to thousands of untimely deaths and is, in fact, reported to being extremely haunted. Based on the countless reports from visitors, every type of strange occurrence imaginable has been reported here. Most commonly, people have claimed to see shadowed figures walking down the long hallways, hearing voices, being touched, and witnessing objects move down the hallway. Quite a large number of children have died at Waverly Hills and it is said that many of them contribute to the haunted activity, which is often said to be of a playful nature. The hallways are littered with toy balls and trucks, due to the reports of visitors getting them to move on command.

It is safe to say that with a resume such as this one, Waverly Hills would be the place that we would ultimately decide to visit. Luckily, the investigation would not be hard to line up, due to the fact that as long as we had ten people who paid one hundred dollars apiece, we would have sole access to the building for eight hours. Of course, everyone wanted to make the trip, so the ten-guest minimum would not be a problem. By this time, Todd had already moved to Texas and formed our sister group, Texas Spirits Paranormal Investigations. I figured we could use some extra help in such a large place so I asked Todd if they wanted to come, in which he quickly took me up on my offer. In addition, I would acquire several new members named Raymond, Jennifer, James, and Carla, all of which have continued to be huge assets to the group.

The planning of the entire event would take several months, as it is always hard to orchestrate the fine details of a large outing involving twenty-five people. As far as transportation, a majority said they were going to carpool for the fourteen hour drive, while several of us decided to fly. I am not the biggest fan of long road trips so I definitely opted for the quick three hour flight. Luckily, most of the group would drive, due to the fact that we had so much equipment to bring. To this day, we have never used that much equipment again, as we would bring four DVR systems, twenty IR cameras, and every EMF meter, voice recorder, and camera we could find. As an added bonus, Todd was able to get his hands on a thermal imaging camera, which we were extremely excited to use. It was safe to say that we were pulling out all the stops in this once in a lifetime opportunity.

After months of anticipation and planning, the day had finally arrived. I made the quick flight to Louisville, Kentucky, and was met at the airport by Brandon and Raymond. We arrived a day early to do a little sightseeing and to hang out with the rest of the group. By that evening, everyone had arrived, so we met for dinner to organize our game plan for the next night. I was so excited; I could hardly keep still, knowing that I would soon be investigating one of the most well-known haunted locations in the country, while additionally, having free roam of the building.

The following day, we were all very eager, knowing that the investigation was only hours away. To kill the time, Raymond took Brandon and me to tour some underground caves, which was quite impressive since caves are something you never see in Louisiana. Speaking of killing, I am still surprised we didn't die that day, since I literally thought Raymond was trying to kill us. Ray is one of the best guys I have ever met, but the poor guy is the worst driver in the world. After our visit to the caves, we stopped at a restaurant for lunch, where Raymond would give one of the best one-liners I have ever heard in my life. After we ate, Ray asked the waitress, "Do you guys have any toothpicks?" After she told him they didn't have any, Ray quickly responded by saying, "I should have figured, we are in Kentucky; you guys don't need toothpicks because you have no teeth to pick." The look on the waitress's face was priceless, as she had no clue what to say. Between Ray's driving and his remarks, I still don't know how we made it back home alive.

Our scheduled time to investigate was 9:00 PM until 5:00 AM and we were told to arrive at Waverly Hills around 8:00 PM, due to the fact that we had to sign liability waivers and such. As we neared the hospital, I could hardly keep still, wondering what the place was going to look like in person. I had seen tons of pictures and video of the hospital, which looked massive, but I had no clue how big it really would be. As we turned down the small gravel road, we began to drive up a small hill. As we topped the hill, there it was. It was truly a picturesque moment, as the sun was setting behind the hospital. The place was freaking enormous. All the pictures I had previously seen did absolutely no justice, as I was immediately intimidated by its size. Ray could not stop the car soon enough, as I couldn't wait to get out and really get a look at the place.

As I exited the vehicle, I was promptly greeted by Donnie, who introduced himself as our tour guide and security for the night. Donnie was a great guy and we were very fortunate to have him as our guide. As expected, everyone rushed out of their vehicles to take pictures of the hospital before it was completely dark. Despite my excitement, our overnight stay had now started, time was money, and we had a million things to do before we could start investigating.

The first matter at hand was how were we going to setup the four DVR systems? We would soon receive the terrible news that in the entire five-story structure, there was only one damn power outlet and it was located on the second floor. As everyone seemed to be more interested in taking a picture in front of the cement gargoyle at the front of the building, Jennifer and I began to brainstorm on how we could get power to all of the floors. After seeing that we had hundreds of feet of extension cords, I decided that the best thing would be to run the cords out of the first, third, and fourth floors and into the second floor where the power outlet was.

Now that the plan was derived, we just had to carry it out. No one seemed understand that we were slowly losing valuable investigating time, causing the good old jerk in me to come out, which often doesn't take that much. After grabbing for a notepad, I quickly broke everyone into four groups of six people, assigning each group to a floor. Each group would then be responsible for setting up a four-camera DVR system on that floor. Once the groups were made and everything was laid out, the group amazingly had the entire building covered with cameras in thirty minutes.

With an hour of our stay already spent, we still had to sign the liability forms prior to the investigation. Donnie took us on a quick tour, as he mentioned some of the hot spots to focus on. Walking through the endless-looking hallways, I couldn't help but imagine all the pain and suffering that had taken place there. As I would look around, I would pause to imagine what it looked like in its former grandeur. Another important thing that I couldn't help but see was the gigantic bats that were flying around. I'm not talking about those tiny little mouse-sized bats you might find in Louisiana; I'm talking about freaking bats that looked like flying cats.

Donnie continued to show us specific points of interest throughout the building, such as the room on the first floor that served as a morgue. In it, there was an autopsy table and the original three-level storage drawers that were used to hold the bodies. Donnie said that it was often a tradition of visitors to lie on one of the drawers and allow themselves to be pushed in the storage area, where voices would often be heard. Without hesitation, I quickly volunteered to try it out later in the night. The rest of the first floor consisted of many distractions, as it also serves as a theatrical haunted house during Halloween. Around every corner, there was some sort of spooky mannequin, which definitely added to the creep factor.

As we made our way to the third and fourth floors, Donnie told us the story of the homeless man and his dog that were reportedly murdered near one of the elevator shafts. He then took us to the small stairwell that led from the third floor to the fourth, where he had a very interesting story. The door that leads to the stairwell is a very solid steel door. We noticed that on the door, there were large gash marks as if someone had struck the door with an axe or some other sharp tool. Donnie went on to say that several years ago, three teenagers had sneaked in the hospital at night. When they made their way past the door, it slammed shut on them. The three began frantically trying to push the door open, yet it would not budge. They then picked up a small axe that they had brought with them and began swinging it at the door, which had no effect. The security guards downstairs were now hearing their cries and screams for help. As the guards approached the door, they observed the three teenagers huddled together, with their faces in the small window of the door, yelling for help. One security guard approached the door and, with one hand, simply opened the door that the three teenagers had tried so diligently to open. The three literally flew out of the doorway and onto the floor. When questioned later as to what they had seen, all they could say was that they saw numerous "shadow people" grabbing at them and would not let them out.

Our brief tour was over and Donnie said that we now had to all leave the hospital and head over to the adjacent laundry building, which is accessible via a short underground tunnel, so we could sign our liability forms. While everyone descended to the first floor, Brandon and I advised Donnie that we would briefly stay behind so we could set up a handheld video camera on the fifth floor. The fifth floor was a partial floor and, ironically, was used to house both the children's' ward and the section for the mentally ill. This level was littered with small toy balls, as it is said to be haunted by a young boy by the name of Timmy. I could not help but get a sense of sadness on this floor, knowing that we were in an area where so many young children had suffered and died at the hands of a merciless disease. I proceeded to set up a video camera on a tripod, facing in the direction of the infamous room 502. I then found a toy ball that someone had left from a previous visit. As I bent down to pick it up, I audibly heard a very distinct voice whisper, "Hey." I quickly turned to Brandon, as he looked behind his own back. Brandon said it was as if the voice came from behind him. I then openly announced to whoever was there that we were not there to cause them any harm. I stated that I was now placing the ball on the ground in front of the camera and if anyone wanted to play with it, they were more than welcomed to once we left. What happened next would truly be amazing. Not to sound macho, but, besides my first visit to Ft. Derussy, I would never get scared during an investigation. However, that would all change with what was about to happen.

By this time, everyone else had made their way to the laundry building next door. Brandon and I were the only two people in the entire five-story structure. We began to make our way down to the fourth floor. As we get in the stairwell between the two floors, Brandon stops to ask me if I realized that we were the only two people in Waverly Hills at that moment. As I paused, we began to hear, what can best be described as four or five children playing tag on the floor that we had just came from. The noise was very loud and distinct, sounding just like several people were running back and forth across the fifth floor. At the same time, Brandon received a substantial spike on his EMF meter. We looked at each other in shock, as neither of us could say a word. In the confusion, we attempted to make our way downstairs, only to find out that we took the wrong set of stairs down. Feeling very disoriented, we attempted to use our two-way radios to get someone to escort us out. However, every time we tried to transmit, we got this extremely strange feedback that I had never heard before on these radios. It was almost as if we were in a game of cat and mouse and we were the hunted. Finally, after several minutes of utter fear and confusion, our trusty pal Raymond came to our rescue, as we were able to join the others for our pre-investigation meeting.

For the actual investigation, we decided to stay in our same groups from earlier in the night, switching floors at timed intervals. Brandon, Raymond, Elissa, and I would initially begin on the third floor. What is unique about the way Waverly Hills is constructed is that the angles in the building allow you to see across to the other side of the building when standing on the solarium. The four of us were all on one end, looking out across to the other side. There were lights behind the building, allowing us to see through it. We were the only team members on the third floor, yet as we peered out, we saw a figure walk in front of one of the lights. We immediately walked down the long hallway to see if anyone was there, but we found no one. With two legitimate experiences in less than an hour, I knew this was going to be one hell of an investigation.

Throughout the night, numerous group members would report strange activity such as unexplainable EMF spikes, strange noises, and glimpses of strange anomalies. In one incident, and investigator attempted to kick one of the balls down the hallways, when he slipped and almost fell over. As this happened, he audibly heard what sounded like a child laugh. Fortunately, he had his voice recorder running at the time and he captured a very clear audio recording of what sounds exactly like a young child laughing.

Of all the experiences had by the numerous visitors of Waverly Hills, the most common are the infamous "shadow people" that are said to walk the long hallways. Prior to the investigation, I was determined to try and debunk the shadow people, figuring the supposed anomalies were caused due to something such as street lights and/or optical illusions. I would have never imagined that I would finally encounter my very own shadow person; however, its origin was not quite as easily explainable as I thought it was going to be.

Several times during the night, while looking down the long hallways, I would see what looked just like peoples' heads poking in and out of the patient's rooms. Of course, the skeptic in me blamed it on my eyes playing tricks on me in the dark. Later that night, Brandon, Elissa, Raymond, and myself would be sitting in one of the hallways, diligently looking across it. In an incident that I would remember for the rest of my life, I suddenly spotted the shadowed silhouette of what looked just like a young girl, approximately eight to ten years old. She had a ponytail and was seen walking out of one room, crossing the hallways, and entering another room. Before I could ever question myself, the four of us all looked at each other in unison, as if to all say, "Did you just see that?" In what probably looked like a pack of stampeding bulls, we all ran down the hallway, only to find that no one was there. I believe that if I would have been the only one who saw the shadow, I probably would have talked myself out of what I thought I saw. However, when there are four people present, simultaneously validating what was witnessed, there must be some legitimacy to the incident.

As the night unfortunately drew closer to an end, I was reminded of another portion of the hospital I wanted to check out. Brandon and I headed down to the first floor to test the claims involving the morgue storage compartments that Donnie had mentioned, which basically looked like large filing cabinets. I decided to go first, as I pulled out the rusty drawer, which let out a chilling screech that sounded like nails on a chalkboard. Simply getting my fat ass on the table was a feat in itself, as I had to jump up on it and lay back in a very awkward position. Once I was lying flat, Brandon shoved the entire drawer back into the compartment. Luckily, I do not suffer from claustrophobia; otherwise I would have been having a fit because the compartment was extremely tight fit, as the ceiling was only several inches from my nose. While in there, I could not help but wonder how many dead bodies had rested on that exact same table. It was completely dark in there, as the soft green light from my K-II meter was the only thing I could see. I lay there motionless, as I stared at the meter. Several seconds later, I looked at my meter and noticed that it had started to give a pretty steady reading of around 5.0 millagauss. What made things so eerie wasn't the fact that I was getting an EMF spike, but the fact that I had nowhere to go. I calmly told Brandon I was ready to get out, so he pulled out the drawer and decided it was his turn. After switching places, I also pushed him completely in the compartment, only after doing so, I stepped out of the room to give the impression that I had left him alone. After calling my name a few times and getting no response, he began to get nervous and in a very distressed tone, he said, "Come on man, this isn't funny, get me out." I know, that was pretty cruel, but I couldn't pass it up.

As daylight was slowly appearing, our investigation was coming to an end. We broke down all of our equipment and began to load everything back in our vehicles. Prior to saying our goodbyes to Donnie, he took us on a walk through the death tunnel. Let me be the first to tell you that if you ever want one of the best workouts in your life, simply walk down and climb back up in the death tunnel. It will wear your butt out. As I mentioned earlier, the tunnel is about five hundred feet long and it is a constant forty-five degree slope the entire way down. We all began walking down it, which wasn't all that bad because we had gravity in our favor. However, my slow walk grew into a brisk walk. My brisk walk grew into a trot, my trot became a jog, and my jog became a run. Next thing I realized, I was uncontrollably running down the tunnel at what seemed to be forty miles an hour. I couldn't stop, as momentum was taking me on a crash course. In a last ditch effort to avoid from completely wiping out, I ran myself into the side of the cement tunnel, which ultimately took all the skin off my arm, yet I didn't bust my ass in front of everyone. After what was probably a record descent of the tunnel, now came the daunting task of climbing back up. Not knowing if it would be easier to use the steps or the ramp, I would soon find out that it really didn't matter which one you used, because when you were done, you would be completely wore out either way. As I finally made my way back up, I could feel my heart pounding in my throat, as I now knew why they called it the death tunnel. It wasn't because they had to transport the death through it, but because once you climbed out of it, you felt like you were about to die.

After taking some final group pictures and saying goodbye to Donnie, we got some well-deserved rest and then prepared for the long trip home. Fortunately, I just had a short plane ride home, while others had to drive back the thirteen hours. Those such as Jennifer, who were confined to a car ride for so long, passed the time by going over the audio recorded during the investigation. Still, as tired as everyone was when the trip was over, I think we would all be more than willing to return to Waverly Hills.

As the days passed, everyone began going over their audio and video. Amazingly, with all of the video we recorded, we were unable to capture anything significant.

In regard to audio, that's a different story. Of all the places we have been and all the quality EVP's we have captured, most of them don't compare to the quality of the ones captured at Waverly Hills. In one of my favorite, James is running audio as he sees a bug and says, "That looks like a firefly." Immediately after he says that, you hear an extremely clear voice of a young boy say, "Yea, it was." In another interesting clip, Elissa and Jennifer are discussing the placement of one of the toy balls. No males were near them, yet as they talk, you can hear a male voice say, "Put that ball down there."

I am often very weary to ever label a location haunted. I will often claim a place to be active, which doesn't necessarily mean it's haunted; it simply means that a place contains some sort of unexplainable activity. However, in one of the few rare cases, I will have to say different, as I will have to join the masses, as I truly feel that Waverly Hills Tuberculosis Sanatorium is definitely haunted. Everyone who attended the investigation came out with some type of personal experiences, all of which were validated by one or more investigators.

With the Waverly Hills investigation out of the way, I began to worry that the other investigations would now all seem mediocre, since we had been to such an active place. Fortunately, it wouldn't be the case, as we tried to handle every case on an individual basis. Sure, we definitely would hit our dry spells, conducting several investigations in a row that produced no evidence, yet that is simply the thrill of the hunt. As I mentioned before, all the dead investigations (no pun intended), would all be worth it when we obtain one piece of valid evidence. However, even with our caseloads, reputation, and recognition continuing to grow, I began to observe ripples in the water. As the saying goes: "Momma ain't raised no fool." I could tell that certain people in the group were starting to act strange, yet I couldn't quite put my finger on it. Fortunately, my instincts would prove to be right, yet I wouldn't be prepared for the way people would decide to carry their selves.

15

DIRTY TACTICS

It is a proven fact that any group must go through some growing pains in order to succeed. I quickly learned at an early point of my ghost hunting tenure, that some of these pains can be a little more intense and last a little longer than others. I began to see that not everyone had as much of a conscience as I did and were often more than willing to lie and deceit. I still never quite understood why people were willing to stoop to such lows in a simple hobby. Why was ghost hunting such a competitive hobby? I would hear horror stories from other groups that even had to seek legal actions, due to the severity of the issues they were having with former members. I would hear things such as individuals sabotaging their former group's investigations, stealing evidence, and all sorts of other dirty mess. I hate to be saying this, but I think it is due to the fact that many individuals who start ghost hunting literally have no lives and they seek any type of action they can find. Some of the most common people I see wanting to join a group, that ultimately fail, are the middle aged women who are either divorced or in a very rough marriage. Many are lonely, want to join some sort of social group, while still doing something a little out of the ordinary. It doesn't make matters any better when they see these different television shows that depict regular people who were fortunate enough to have their own show. These are often the individuals that like to start rumors, simply to see dissension among the ranks for the mere fact that they must live for drama.

As I mentioned earlier, one of the biggest catalysts for tension amongst a group is that fact that paranormal investigating attracts such an eclectic group of personalities into a centralized area. These different personalities quickly clash over a wide array of topics ranging from religious beliefs to simple evidence analysis. The one thing that I learned quick when running my own group is that you will never please everyone. No matter what type of group structure you operate, there will always be at least one complainer in the group that nothing seems to please. There is no soothing these individuals, as the best thing you can do is run your group in the most efficient of manners that can accompany as many members of your group as possible. The nay-sayers will either conform to everyone else or simply fall to the wayside.

However, like I said, ghost hunting does not always attract the most honest and good-hearted people around, which is why it is so hard to maintain a good reputation with the general public. Let's face it; we have all dealt with useless people in a group that have not only wasted you and your group's time, but also jeopardized its existence by bringing unneeded drama into the circle. Most of the valid investigators out there deal with enough headaches in their home and work lives, and do not need that type of worry in a hobby that is supposed to serve as a form of relaxation. I have lost good people before, simply due to the fact that they didn't want to be around the negativity of a poor investigator. These investigators are also a threat because they often enjoy spreading their misery to as many others as possible, just so they cannot feel alone.

Beginning with LGH, I dealt with people such as Mr. Personality, who didn't have a happy bone in their body. This would continue on with LaSpirits; as we would have numerous members come and go who simply seemed to cause trouble. On the positive side, it has caused me to now be much stricter in the selection process of new members. The best advice I can give groups who are having the same problem is to not hype up your group when speaking with a potential member. I find you weed out a majority of the crap when you basically bring out all the negatives first, such as the long hours of traveling, the possibility of many boring investigations, and the fact that they must put this over the priority of other extracurricular activities. Many people that contact a legitimate group have the misconceptions that they are only a small, fly-by-night group that meets once every few months in a cemetery for a quick scare. I notice that by letting them immediately know that is not the case and we are extremely structured and require much of their time, they don't even bother contacting you again. Ultimately, this is good because they do not waste your time any further and you quickly weed out those that are lazy and do not want to put forth any effort.

However, there will always be those snakes in the grass that make it on the team and do a good job for quite some time. These people cause you to actually trust and befriend them, as they seem like good individuals. Unfortunately, they are only putting up a smoke screen and their charades eventually stop, exposing them for the real jerks they really are. These are the most dangerous to deal with, as they are capable of committing the dirtiest of tactics for the simple fact that they have no morals and thrive on deceit.

During the period just prior to the Waverly Hills investigation, I truly felt that we had a very strong group that all seemed to work in unison. All four chapters were working hard, obtaining some big investigations. There was one member of the group, who I will call Tom, which had been with me from day one of the LGH days. We were great friends, hanging out every chance we could. We would help each other out during several of our tough times, constantly staying in touch. The one negative thing about Tom was that no matter how much I tried to become close friends with him, he always seemed to have some sort of secret vendetta against me. I would often catch wind of incidents where he would vent his unknown frustration with me, yet when I would confront him, he would always deny that there were never any problems. One of Tom's flaws was that he seemed to enjoy being the whipping boy, always complaining about not feeling important in the group, yet he never put forth the effort to accomplish anything that would allow him to receive any credit. Despite his flaws and his sporadic snide remarks behind my back, I always brushed them off, as I continued to assume that we were good friends, putting forth all the effort I could give in keeping a close relationship.

One of my other chapters consisted of several investigators who, despite the fact that they were hard working and lined up some great investigations, seemed to live for drama and had absolutely no loyalty to one another. Every week consisted of a different qualm about one another. In one week, member "A" would say how much they couldn't stand member "B". The following week, members "A" and "B", who had now made amends, were complaining about how much they hated member "C". This went on week in and week out, as I tried my best to ignore the entire thing, due to the fact that as long as they were still getting good investigations, I really didn't care what they thought of one another, especially since their thoughts of one another would fluctuate weekly. I do not have much personal regard for people who act like that, as it is extremely difficult to deal with two-faced individuals.

Despite all the quirks, the job was getting done and there was nothing more I could do. In preparation of the trip to Waverly, we had all agreed that once we all arrived, we would get together and have dinner. As we arrived in Kentucky, we all began to contact one another to arrange a meeting point. Tom and the "Three Stooges" that I mentioned earlier, were the only ones that did not seem to want to get together. Once we arrived, they all seemed like they had some sort of excuse on why they couldn't meet. The three days we were there, they seemed to be very elusive and all were acting extremely odd. It was as if they were now forming a strange clique, consisting of people who all had run each others' names through the shredder on a regular basis. Things were not adding up, yet I decided to put it in the back of my head for the moment, as we had a huge investigation to conduct. To give you an example of how elusive the members were being, it wasn't until the second day I was there, that I learned that they were actually staying in the same hotel as me, on the same floor, five rooms down.

Arriving at Waverly Hills would be the first time I would see Tom in the two days that we had been in town. There was a quirkiness about him that evening I couldn't quite put my finger on, and it didn't help matters any when I noticed that the Stooges stayed to themselves the entire night of the investigation. During the investigation, Tom continuously complained about how he could have saved his time and money by going to one of the haunted plantations in Louisiana. His negativity was beginning to bring everyone around him down that night, as those in his group were trying their best to avoid him. In one instance, an investigator asked him if they could take a break so she could use the bathroom, in which he rudely denied her request. Looking at Tom, it was obvious that something was up with him and he didn't even want to be there. The nail in the coffin was once the investigation was over. It was about 6:00 AM and we all had packed our equipment up and proceeded to take a final group photo, standing in front of the hospital. Our intentions were to all go back to our hotel rooms and get a few hours of sleep before the trip home. As we told our goodbyes to the tour guide, we then began wishing each other a safe trip back. Just then, I turned to look for Tom and the Stooges so I could tell them bye and all I saw was the rear taillights from their vehicles, as they sped off the grounds. I could not believe that they had been so blatantly rude, that they simply left without telling anyone goodbye. It would take several days to get in touch with them and when I asked their reasons why they left so abruptly, they all gave the lame excuse that they were tired. I knew something was up and it was only a matter of time before the ugly truth would float to the surface.

Prior to the trip, Brandon and I had constantly been having trouble with one of Tom's members, as he showed absolutely no urge to participate whatsoever. We would go months without hearing from him, he would never make any investigations, and he ultimately showed no interest in being an asset to the group. On numerous occasions, we had conferred with Tom regarding the possibility of removing the guy from the group, yet Tom insisted that they were very good friends and he was working on things that he just wasn't telling the group. Per Tom's requests, we continued to leave his friend in the group, although his participation and visibility seemed to worsen instead of improving. One of the hardest things about running a group that is as structured as ours is that you must be willing to differentiate friends from effective group members. If you are that serious in seeing your group succeed, you must have only members who will show an interest in being in the group. If they are legitimately your close friends, they should respect where you are coming from and not blow a gasket when you tell them that they need to improve their performance or they will be removed from the group.

After we returned from Waverly, the member's participation continued to deteriorate. Ultimately, we had no choice but to send him a polite e-mail, informing him that due to his habitual lack of communication and interest in the group, he was being removed from the group. I forwarded a copy to Tom, which ended up being the icing on the cake. I had the notion that Tom was going to be enraged because he was not included in the decision. He already had the habit of getting upset when he wasn't made to feel important, so I knew he would blow up. However, I was at the point that I had a group to run and was tired of walking on eggshells to stroke people's egos. I assumed that if we were as good friends as I thought we were, Tom would respect that and realize I was looking out for the best interests of the group. Unfortunately, I quickly learned that when you assume things, you quickly make an "ass" out of "you" and "me".

Several hours after I removed Tom's friend from the group, I received an e-mail from Tom, simply stating that he was quitting the group due to personal issues. I immediately called him to see what was going on. He initially tried to beat around the bush, saying that he quit because of money and time restraints, but later admitted that it was due to his friend being removed from the group. I knew of his personality and knew that it wouldn't pay to try and coerce him back in the group. I was more upset than anything, as it appeared as if he had taken our friendship, which seemed to be faux from the beginning, and literally discarded it with no remorse.

Despite the considerable loss to the group, we still had to carry on as usual. By this time, Jennifer had began to show huge improvements in her performance and quickly showed that she had the leadership abilities and the drive to fill in the void. To this day, Jennifer is my "right hand gal", running the show when I take an often-needed break from things. What would happen next would only solidify the strange behavior of Tom and the Stooges back in Waverly.

Within days of Tom resigning from the group, I began receiving e-mails from the Stooges, claiming that they were receiving anonymous messages from someone, making ridiculous claims that they were going to be removed from the group and that I was stealing group funds. The members stated that they were beginning to get tired of getting harassed and were contemplating leaving the group. Things were just not adding up due to the fact that when I would try and question them on the details of the messages and where the address was coming from, they all began to dance around the subject. One of the members then had the gall to falsely admit that the messages were coming from a former member of our group. As I continued to interrogate the Stooges on the source of these e-mails, they continued to vaguely talk about it, causing me to feel that these claims were simply a cop-out to allow their selves to graciously leave the group.

In the meantime, Tom, who had adamantly professed that he was not going to continue ghost hunting, crawls from the woodworks with a fully functioning Website, representing his new group. His departure had only been days before the erection of the site, causing me to believe that the site was being worked on way before he quit. Another thing that looked suspicious was that the style of the Website's design strongly matched several other sites that were made by one of the Stooges. Could this have been one huge ploy, originated way before Waverly? It would only make perfect sense, especially after the apparent change in personalities during the trip.

I then took my speculations to one of the Stooges, asking them what was all going on. It didn't take long for him to admit that they had been working on this site for a while and were looking at a way to break the news. Although upset, I remained civil, as I wished the Stooges the best of luck with their new group, even offering my assistance if they ever needed. I even went as far as adding one of their Website banners to my site, advertising their existence.

In a pathetic act of deceitfulness, closely mimicking the actions carried out by the individual at the Gothic Jail, Tom began to "bite the hand that fed him", spreading the accusations that I had been stealing group funds, as well as all other sorts of ridiculous accusations. Needless to say, I was furious, yet being the God-fearing man I am, I decided to turn the other check and simply remove their banner from our website, attempting to wipe my hands clean of the whole ordeal. I refused to stoop to the levels of these individuals, as it was apparent that they were so devious, they would stab their own mothers in the back without an ounce of remorse. What was even more ridiculous was that they then had the nerve to act as if they were upset when I removed their banner from my site. They then felt in was necessary to take the amount of mud-slinging a step further by now trying to turn my current members on me. Luckily, the group that I now had knew that their accusations were simply lies, paying them no mind.

By this time, it was taking every bit of humility I had not to act out, yet I continued to simply fester in my own anger. The new group had now begun editing their website to nearly mimic mine, yet at the same time, trying to tarnish our name in every way that they could. To this day, I still can't figure out how openly hypocritical someone can be by blatantly plagiarizing someone's work, while running the names of others in the ground. I have often heard that imitation is the best form of flattery, but these guys were taking it to the next level.

Beginning to see how low these cowards were willing to stoop, I began to put myself in their shoes, trying to predict their next move. Seeing how they were obviously trying to hit way below the belt, it was apparent that they were trying to ruin the most important things to me in the paranormal community. One of our proudest accomplishments has been that we are the Louisiana representatives for a very popular, nationwide investigative group, handling all Louisiana-based caseloads for them. The Stooges knew how much this recognition meant to me, so what better way to ultimately get at me than to try and have that label taken from me.

I decided that the best thing was to try and beat them to the punch, so I contacted the two managers of the representative family. I basically ran down the situation to them, advising them that even though they may not try anything, I was simply putting a bug in their ears. One of the managers began to laugh, saying that it was funny I mentioned that since he had, in fact, received an email several days earlier. The e-mail was from an individual, claiming to be one of our former clients. Below is a copy of the actual message that was originally written:

"Hi my name is Jake and I saw that LaSpirits was a member of your group, so I trusted them to come do an investigation at my home. My kids are being bothered at night to the point where I am thinking about moving. These people came to my home drunk and one of them was so drunk he went to

the bathroom on his self. The others were cussing some foul words; my 3 kids were home at this time. I can't believe you would let people like this in your group. I asked them to leave and the founder told me he did not have to do nothing because he was a member of your group. I have talked to several people that they have done investigations for and they were not happy either. Because of this, I will never trust in your organization again and will make sure no one I know does either. Thank you, Jake Dawson."

When I first read the e-mail, I was unsure as to laugh or kick somebody's butt. It was obvious that the message was a complete hoax, yet I couldn't fathom why someone would stoop so low. For starters, we have never had a client named Jake Dawson, and the address that was given, which was supposed to be located in Pineville, is not even a valid street name in that city. The kicker that really gave it all away, proving that we weren't dealing with smartest of people, was the e-mail address that the message was sent from. The address contained five digits, resembling a Louisiana zip code. With the aid of a zip code locater, it was learned that the zip actually belonged to the very small town where all three of the Stooges lived. It was safe to say that this was all a little too coincidental to simply brush off.

Luckily, the managers that I had contacted could easily see through the phoniness of the message. They both reassured me that no one was going to take the e-mail serious and our status in the organization was just as strong as ever. However, the severity of their intentions was apparent and I truly witnessed what low-life pieces of crap I had been dealing with all along. I forwarded Jake Dawson's e-mail to Tom, allowing him to see what type of antics his members were up to. Of course, Tom denied any knowledge of what was done, yet I could tell he was lying through his teeth. I proceeded to tell Tom how one of the Stooges claimed that they received harassing e-mails from a former member of ours. Again, Tom denied knowledge of this and went as far as trashing the name of the former member, saying how he would never have any dealings with her again. Amazingly, about a month later, guess who was added to their website as a new member? You guessed it; the former member Tom and the Stooges had all bashed on numerous occasions. Once again, proof that there is absolutely no honor amongst thieves. It is quite ironic to know that the group consists of individuals that are all guilty of talking endless amounts of crap about one another in the past, yet all of a sudden, they seem to act as if they are now best of friends.

These days, the trouble makers have seemed to cease their antics, yet I often like to say that I am like a midget in a urinal; I am always on my toes. After seeing how low people that I thought were my friends were willing to stoop, nothing seems to surprise me anymore. However, there were several benefits that came out of these unfortunate events. The first advantage was that I had symbolically flushed the toilet in the group, getting rid of all the waste that would eventually cause me more problems. The second benefit was that I truly feel that I became a more efficient leader after dealing with the unfortunate antics. I now had a much more defined mission statement for the group and now had a stronger ability to deal with the different personalities in the group. However, due to our selection process, which has now become even stricter, we have been very fortunate in bringing in some very hard working, level-headed, and similar individuals that all have the same goal in mind.

To this day, we try our best to have the best possible rapport with groups inside of the state. However, as we have seen, no matter how much you try to be civil with some; there are always those who will have an unknown grudge against you and your group. Not to sound conceited, but I think a majority of the hostility originates from plain old jealousy. I have often seen individuals such as Tom and the guy at the Gothic Jail, who are incapable of bettering themselves, take the easy way out and try to bring others down to their level of underachievement. Whether it is due to incompetence or laziness, these types of people find it easier to whine and complain, as opposed to achieving success.

By this point in the book, you should now see why I take so much pride in the group. By going through so much headache and drama, I have proven that I am pretty much capable of overcoming any group-related issues. Don't get me wrong, there are many times where I feel overwhelmed, wondering if all the crap I have dealt with is really worth continuing on with the group. It is these times when I remember that if I do decide to disband the group, then I would simply allow those such as Tom to succeed in their dirty tactics. I refuse to allow people such as that to feel that they have the upper hand on me, stressing me out so much that I wipe my hands clean of the entire hobby, throwing all of my hard work away. I will never guarantee that I will investigate forever, but I do promise that I will not quit until I truly feel that I no longer have anything left to offer to the hobby. I will call it quits only when I feel it is time; not when idiots such as the ones I have dealt with so many times over, think they have stressed me out to the point of disbandment.

I would like to think that all of the rough times are past us now. I have matured enough to let many of the remarks go in one ear and out the other. Things that would have once sent me in a rage, doesn't quite affect me the same way anymore. I am quite secure with the fact that we are currently the most successful group in the state, landing some of the largest investigations around, while continuing to educate the public in how we conduct our investigations. We have begun to offer Continuing Education courses at numerous accredited universities in the state, all of which have become tremendously popular. My security has caused me not to feel that there is need for any sort of competition amongst groups, as we stay way too busy to worry about such asinine behavior. Groups that are worried about stirring the pot within the community are simply spinning their wheels in the mud, wasting their own time, while further running their own name into the ground. In the meantime, we continue to "kick ass and take names."

16
WHAT THE FUTURE HOLDS

I often wonder how much longer I will actually continue on with the group. Who knows, by the time this book is published, I may be long gone from the paranormal community. Regardless of what happens, I can honestly say that I have given it my all, forming a legitimate group made up of some great people. Sure, there have been many bumps along the way, but I really feel that it was all necessary in order to grow and mature into what we have become. As I said, the group has also helped me mature personally, greatly increasing my interpersonal communication skills and leadership abilities.

I would like to think that one of our biggest accomplishments was that we simply brought some normality to the hobby within the state. In our few years of existence we have proved to the public that you do not have to look like a vampire to be a legitimate paranormal investigator. For quite some time, we have broken through the stereotypical barriers, showing that normal people with normal lives can be part of a strange hobby, while actually being taken serious by skeptics and media alike.

When I started writing this book, my main goal was to accommodate to as wide of a range of readers as possible, covering every possible angle of this hobby that I could think of. Most books that I have come across seemed so serious and lacked the personality that your "Average Joe" could relate to. I wanted a book that could relate to everyone from the newest of investigators, all the way to the seasoned investigators and history buffs that want to get a good look at historical haunts across the state.

My greatest bridge to cross was to give a raw look at what was really involved in paranormal investigating. I wanted to expose the dirt that many groups were afraid to talk about, for fear that the topics were a bit too taboo or that they felt that they were actually guilty of the very same things. It was not always easy to recollect all the harsh incidents that I have experienced, yet I felt it was all necessary for people to really see how ridiculous others can act. What has always been ironic is that those who disguise themselves as the straight-line walking, hard core investigators are always the ones that have proven to be guilty of being the overly competitive, backstabbing individuals that have caused me so much trouble over time. It reminds me of many of the bible-thumbing holy rollers out there that are actually some of the most crooked people around.

It is interesting to ponder for a moment on when the ghost hunting fad will come to an end. When all the television shows have gone off the air for good, what will be left of the thousands of investigative groups across the country? What will happen to all those in the hobby that were merely in it for the potential of fame? What would happen if someone would find definitive proof that the paranormal exist? Would the thrill of the hunt be as intense? These are all questions we must ask ourselves sooner or later. We all know that nothing last forever and neither will ghost hunting. Maybe I will reach the point where what once interested me is not substantial enough to cause me to work so hard to continue doing. Only time will tell where fate will take me. Then again, I may just make millions on this book, retire, and never have to lift a finger again. I hope you noticed the sarcasm in that remark.

Looking back on things, despite the entire headache, I don't think I would change a single thing. Everything that I've been through, positive or negative, has been a learning experience. I have visited some of the most historical locations in and around the state; places that I would have never dreamed of visiting if I wouldn't have gotten involved with paranormal investigating. I have met some awesome people, as well as stone cold pieces of crap, yet they have all played a part in some way or another, in regards to the success of my group.

Even if I decide to depart from the paranormal scene one day, I would ultimately love to see Louisiana Spirits live on. I often joke with Jennifer, telling her, "Someday this will all be yours." She often takes it as a joke, but I know that I will not do this forever, and I honestly feel that Jennifer possesses the leadership and the determination to see that the group continues to flourish. With the help of all my other hard-working members, I can legitimately see the group prospering, even once I am gone.

To all of you, I thank you for taking the time to read a project of mine that has long been in the works. I really hope this book served as an informative read, giving a fresh look and feel to what has unfortunately become a boring and monotonous subject at times. I especially hope that this read was of use to those who are interested in either joining an investigating group or starting their own, as I have tried my best to let you know what can really lurk in the shadows once you go "lights out."

To those who unfortunately related a little too much with this book, it is never too late to change for yourself and for those you have been crude to. If you thought the things that I mentioned were tasteless and harsh, I apologize, yet we all know that the truth hurts sometimes. What is really sad, is that there were many other things that I could have wrote about, but to save face and avoid legal retribution, I had to tone things down a bit. I probably could have added another three or four chapters, simply by exposing the other things that went on that I couldn't discuss. All I can say is that for a group to remain credible they really must carefully screen who they let in, for many of these individuals may be thieves, liars, and even drug addicts. These are definitely not the sort of people who you want around, for they quickly infect the quality of your group. Not to mention, who wants to get pulled over by the cops for speeding, not knowing that someone riding with you has an eight-ball of "blow" on them?

In closing, the best thing I can tell you is to simply have fun. Despite everything I have preached, if you don't have the time to devote yourself to a structured organization, just grab a camera, flashlight, voice recorder, and a few friends and head to the nearest cemetery. Regardless of what some might think, my intentions were not to deter anyone from investigating, but to give as real of a look into a fascinating hobby that has strangely become mainstream. Again, I hope I was able to bring you a non-traditional, yet informative and entertaining book, regarding my true passion. If anyone ever has any questions, please e-mail me at bduplechien@laspirits.com. Thank you, God Bless, and always remember LaSpirits's motto:

—*"Ghost Hunters Do it in the Dark."*

REFERENCES

Amort, J. (n.d.). *About Us: Oak Alley Plantation*. Retrieved April 4, 2008, from Oak Alley Plantation: http://www.oakalleyplantation.com/about/history/

Coleman, E. (2005). *Louisiana Haunted Forts*. Lanham, Maryland: Taylor Trade Publishing.

History of the Municipal. (n.d.). Retrieved April 8, 2008, from Shreveport Municipal Memorial Auditorium: http://www.stageofstars.com/history.html

History: Rip Van Winkle Gardens. (n.d.). Retrieved April 9, 2008, from Rip Van Winkle Gardens: http://www.ripvanwinklegardens.com/rvwgardens.asp

Mohsenifar, Z. (n.d.). *Tiburculosis Symptons, Cause, Transmission, Diagnosis, and Treatment*. Retrieved April 19, 2008, from MedicineNet: http://www.medicinenet.com/tuberculosis/article.htm

Saxon, L., & Tallant, R. (1945). *Gumbo Ya-Ya: Folk Tales of Louisiana*. Gretna, La: Pelican Publishing Co.

Smith, S. (n.d.). *Oakland Cemetery*. Retrieved April 9, 2008, from Haunted Louisiana: http://www.hauntla.com/oakland.html

Viviano, C. L. (1992). *Haunted Louisiana*. Metairie, La: Tree House Press.

Waverly Hills Sanatorium. (n.d.). Retrieved April 19, 2008, from http://waverlyhillstbsanatorium.com

WEBSITES

Paranormal Groups/Informative Sites:

Louisiana Spirits Paranormal Investigations (www.laspirits.com)
Texas Spirits Paranormal Investigations (www.txspirits.com)
Seekers of Unexplained Louisiana (www.soul-online.org)
The Atlantic Paranormal Society (www.the-atlantic-paranormal-society.com)
The TAPS Family (www.tapsfamily.com)
Oklahoma Paranormal Researchers and Investigations (www.okpri.com)
Oklahoma City Ghost Club (www.okcgc.net)
Arkansas PAST (www.arpast.org)
Haunted Louisiana (www.hauntedla.com)
Ghost Vigil (www.ghostvigil.com)
American Paranormal Investigations (www.ap-investigations.com)
The Shadowlands (www.theshadowlands.net)
Skeptical Analysis of the Paranormal Society (www.skepticalanalysis.com)
Southern California Paranormal Research Society (www.socalprs.com)
About Paranormal (www.paranormal.about.com)
Oak Alley Plantation (www.oakalleyplantation.com)
Loyd's Hall Plantation (www.loydhall.com)
Joseph Jefferson Mansion (www.ripvanwinklegardens.com)
Babel Con Sci-Fi Convention (www.babelcon.org)
Shreveport Municipal Auditorium (www.stageofstars.com)

Paranormal Equipment Sites:

    Less EMF (www.lessemf.com)
    Closeout CCTV (www.closeoutcctv.com)
    Raiden Tech (www.raidentech.com)
    Ghost Mart (www.ghost-mart.com)
    Flir Thermal Imaging (www.flir.com)

978-0-595-51265-2
0-595-51265-8

Printed in the United States
126266LV00003B/257/P